FIVE DAYS

BALTIMORE'S FIERY RECKONING

WES MOORE WITH ERICA L. GREEN

ICON

Published in the UK in 2021
by Icon Books Ltd, Omnibus Business Centre,
39–41 North Road, London N7 9DP
email: info@iconbooks.com
www.iconbooks.com

First published in the USA in 2020
by One World, an imprint of Random House,
a division of Penguin Random House LLC, New York.

Sold in the UK, Europe and Asia
by Faber & Faber Ltd, Bloomsbury House,
74–77 Great Russell Street,
London WC1B 3DA or their agents

Distributed in the UK, Europe and Asia
by Grantham Book Services, Trent Road, Grantham NG31 7XQ

Distributed in Australia and New Zealand
by Allen & Unwin Pty Ltd,
PO Box 8500, 83 Alexander Street,
Crows Nest, NSW 2065

Distributed in South Africa
by Jonathan Ball, Office B4, The District,
41 Sir Lowry Road, Woodstock 7925

Distributed in India by Penguin Books India,
7th Floor, Infinity Tower – C, DLF Cyber City,
Gurgaon 122002, Haryana

ISBN: 978-178578-724-9

Designed by Caroline Cunningham

Printed and bound in Great Britain
by Clays Ltd, Elcograf S.p.A.

To Mia, James, and all of the children of Baltimore.

I believe in you. And we will do better.

Prologue

I SAT IN THE FARTHEST PEW from the front in a Baltimore chapel, staring at the flawless ivory-colored casket of a twenty-five-year-old man. Afraid to go any closer. Wondering why I was even this close. High above his casket on the back wall of the chapel, the words "Black Lives Matter" were projected onto a screen, as if the aspirational slogan and the body below were not statements in violent contradiction.

It was the morning of Monday, April 27, 2015, and I was at Freddie Gray's funeral. Three weeks earlier, on April 12, 2015, a police officer on a bicycle had made eye contact with the still-living Freddie Gray, a young man from the Sandtown-Winchester/Harlem Park section of Baltimore—the "wrong side" of Baltimore, a neighborhood where life expectancy was not quite sixty-five years, a full seven years shorter than in the rest of Baltimore and around the same as someone living in North Korea. Gray met the officer's eyes and ran. The officer gave chase, soon joined by two others, and soon Gray was captured. The police searched him, and when they found a pocketknife in his pocket, they arrested him. When he couldn't, or wouldn't, walk to their transport van, they dragged him along the sidewalk. What happened next was a matter of dispute. But when Freddie Gray died a week later, from a severed spine, much of Baltimore believed the police had killed him.

That belief didn't come out of nowhere. What was life like if you grew up like Freddie Gray? The fear of being a victim of police brutality was ever present if you were young and black in Baltimore—just one more trial for kids who already carried the mental anguish and physical adversity of growing up in chronically neglected neighborhoods. You knew neighbors, cousins, uncles, aunties, and friends who'd been victims of random or targeted violence. The violence was physical but correlated with the emotional violence that was often its cause or consequence. And the violence was pervasive, a factor in every decision you made—which streets you walked down, what time you started and ended your day, whom you trusted. The most quotidian decisions were shaped by structurally determined abnormalities. You called it life.

In that chaos, you feel a need to rely on the institutions that supposedly are in place to support you and your family: your school, your place of worship, your city government, your fire department, your police department. The individuals who make up these institutions pledged to uphold your best interests and safety, to protect and serve. But what happens when those pledges are broken, when those institutions break down? What happens when it no longer feels like the schools are deepening your education or preparing you for work? What happens when houses of worship feel void of spirituality and unresponsive to your everyday needs? What happens when your political representatives seem to be more concerned with the interests of the wealthy and already powerful and are careless or contemptuous in the face of genuine human pain and distress? And what happens when the people who are paid to protect you are your predators? Your institutions of support become your captors. Your saviors become your jailers.

Freddie Gray and so many other boys like him grew up in the type of poverty that permeates everything: how you are educated, the water you drink, the home you live in, the air you breathe, the school you spend most of your day in, the way you are policed, whether or not you will die in the same poverty you were born in. It was that poverty that raised the probability that Freddie would be exactly where he was on April 12, 2015, and then again on April 27, 2015. In fact, the odds started being stacked against Freddie generations before he was born.

Harvard economists Raj Chetty and Nathaniel Hendren released a report right before Freddie Gray was arrested for the final time. The report compiled years of research on the best and worst places in America for young children born into poverty to grow up. Many of the best places were in the DMV area—the District of Columbia, Maryland, and Virginia—including Montgomery County, Maryland, a jurisdiction that hugs the nation's capital and consistently has the highest-rated schools in the state of Maryland. Montgomery County is also a little more than twenty-five miles from the jurisdiction that Chetty and Hendren reported as the worst place in the country to be born poor: the city of Baltimore, Freddie Gray's place of birth.

For every year of his life spent in Baltimore, the report stated, a poor boy's earnings as an adult would fall by 1.5 percent. When you factor that in for an entire childhood and early adulthood, the average twenty-six-year-old man who grew up poor in Baltimore would earn about 28 percent less than if he grew up anywhere else in the country. But why?

It's not an accident. Poverty is so concentrated because it is generational and, research shows, created with relentless intention. Redlining, predatory lending and discriminatory covenants, blockbusting, and forced segregation all constrained opportunities and cut off pathways to increased material and social capital for generations of black Baltimoreans. Transportation lines were drawn to prevent these communities' access to jobs and services—and, just as importantly, to keep the haves and have-nots separated. Underfunded and poorly managed schools failed to serve as engines of economic mobility for families. Talented teachers and administrators were provided greater incentives to move on than to stay on. The same applied to students, who dropped out at alarming rates—and even the ones who graduated from a Baltimore high school did so largely unprepared for higher education or employment.

I am from Baltimore but run the largest poverty-fighting organization in New York City—one of the largest in the country. I spend a great deal of time in economically distressed communities in New York: Brownsville, East New York, the South Bronx. These places are nationally known, statistically and anecdotally, for their significant challenges when it comes to creating true and sustainable economic mobility. New York in no way has poverty defeated. The life expectancy in Brownsville, Brooklyn, is seven years shorter than the average life expectancy in the city as a whole. The South Bronx neighborhoods of Mott Haven and Melrose have three times as many hospitalizations for asthma as the rest of the city. But the truth is I would rather be born poor in New York than in Baltimore.

That morning in April, when we gathered to lay Freddie Gray to rest, protests in Baltimore surrounding his killing had been going on for weeks and showed no signs of quieting; in fact, they seemed to be gaining in intensity. The silence from the police department and elected officials in the face of Freddie's suspicious death was met by screams from the other side, demanding answers and accountability.

The funeral took place on a clear spring day in Baltimore. Just forty-eight hours before, the city had erupted in violence and vandalism. So, as they prepared to bury Freddie, elected officials and the Gray family asked for peace. Congressman Elijah Cummings, who represented the 7th Congressional District in Baltimore, Freddie Gray's home district, made this plea before the funeral: "I haven't come here to ask you to respect the wishes of the family. I've come here to beg you."

I arrived early to the New Shiloh Baptist Church, early enough that there were only hundreds of people there, not the thousands who would eventually converge on the church that morning. I hadn't been to New Shiloh in years, but it was the church I'd attended back when I was a student. I'd walked its center aisle on the day the senior pastor invited visitors who were looking for a church home to come forward, a cherished ritual in the black church tradition. As I walked down the aisle that day—along with a half dozen other new members— people cheered, prayed, and clapped. The church community saw our journey down that aisle as proof of the potency and durability of Jesus's message of liberation. On this day thousands more would walk down that aisle, not to give their lives to a higher purpose but to remember a life that had been taken away.

I didn't join the procession to pay respects but watched the community as it poured down that aisle. Some men and women were in T-shirts, others in mourning black. The politicians began to arrive, a who's who of Baltimore political power

walking into the sanctuary and proceeding down the aisle toward the open casket. I sat in the back, conflicted about
whether my presence there was meaningful or right. I wanted
to pay my respects, but I didn't feel I deserved to take that
walk. I have attended many funerals in my life. Funerals of
family and friends and siblings of friends from my old neighborhood. Battlefield funerals in Afghanistan and stateside remembrances of soldiers who paid the highest price. But this
was the first funeral I had ever attended of someone I didn't
know in life—someone whose name I didn't even know until
his death. And that was the problem.

While Gray's premature death touched me deeply, what I
was coming to know of his life bothered me more. We had
come from similar places, but I had been so fortunate, so
blessed. So lucky. I had a mom who didn't understand "no" and
who had creative resources around her that helped keep our
family afloat and on the move. I was lucky that my run-ins
with law enforcement at a young age weren't fatal or trauma-
tizing. Lucky that I was given the opportunity to have second
chances. Our family had ambition and were wildly opportunis-
tic when openings appeared—but luck and circumstance were
on our side, too.

In the back of that sanctuary, I pondered the details I knew
of Freddie's life. I'd learned that he had been poisoned by lead
as a toddler: his family was part of a lawsuit against a property
owner over Freddie and his siblings' exposure to unsafe levels
of lead, a neurotoxin that causes damage to the brain in many
ways, from learning disabilities to a propensity for aggression.
Five micrograms of lead in a deciliter of blood is the point at
which negative impacts are predicted. Thirty-six micrograms
were found in Freddie's blood. These children—including
Freddie—were born into homes and neighborhoods that were

literally making them sick. He never held a legal job for long and had done time for petty crimes. The officers who arrested him that April day knew him by name.

Sitting in the back of the chapel, I meditated on his painful life—or what I knew of it—and its painful end. And I prayed for his family, who were weathering public scrutiny after having become national symbols of police violence, a position they weren't prepared for. Then I sat looking around the church at all the civic leaders beginning to gather near the sanctuary's pulpit. Was this just theater? Or would this solemn gathering effect change on a scale that was commensurate with the loss—the losses—we were marking? Did we even know what that kind of change would look like?

I left before the eulogy, the soaring speeches, and the tear-jerking remembrances. I had to catch a flight to Boston for a speech I was giving—on poverty. I was thirty thousand feet in the air when it became clear to the world that the funeral would not be the big news of the day. The city I called home, the city that had helped raise me, was about to come under siege.

I had been invited to Boston not just because I was at the time directing an anti-poverty educational organization that I founded, but because of my own life history: after being raised by a single mother and coming of age in Baltimore and the Bronx, I was being presented as a "success story." My story let people believe that individual effort could overcome obstacles, so they wouldn't have to think too hard about the systems, structures, and policies that make stories like mine so rare. I was starting to realize that basking in this kind of celebration was its own kind of problem—that it made me complicit in a

kind of blindness. I was thinking about all of this while hur-
tling toward Boston at thirty thousand feet, but I didn't realize
just how far removed from the ground I was.

Before I got off the plane, back in Baltimore things had escalated. It was during those few hours that young people and
police faced off at Mondawmin Mall, rocks flew, and officers
were hurt. Mondawmin Mall, a three-level shopping center,
sits in the heart of West Baltimore. It was also a central transportation hub, and that became part of the story later in the
afternoon, when buses and trains in and around Mondawmin
were shut down by the city; many people blamed that action
for the escalation in violence that followed. By the time my
plane landed in Boston, my voicemail was full of frantic calls
from friends and family and requests from media colleagues to
come on the air and talk about what was happening in our city.
I went to my hotel and sat up most of the night talking to
loved ones and watching cable news, piecing together as best I
could what was happening.

When I was four, my father died in front of me in our Maryland home. Afterward, we moved to the Bronx and lived with
my grandparents on crack-plagued and police-harassed streets
in a neighborhood that many felt had intentionally been allowed to descend into squalor and chaos. The Bronx helped to
shape me and build me. By the time I was eleven I knew the
feeling of handcuffs on my wrists. By thirteen I had been
placed on academic and disciplinary probation at my school.

My mother had eventually found a good job in New York—
the first job that had ever given her full benefits (life and health
insurance as well as retirement), the first job that paid her
enough that she didn't need a second one to raise her three

children, the first job that would give her regular hours. The Annie E. Casey Foundation is one of the nation's largest philanthropies with a focus on children, with close to $1 billion in assets. The endowment was established by one of the founders of United Parcel Service and named after his mother. When my mother got a job there, the foundation was headquartered in Greenwich, Connecticut, an affluent enclave outside of New York City, and she commuted an hour and a half each way. But two years after she was hired, the organization's board decided to move to an area that more closely aligned with the work they were focusing on. They chose to move to Baltimore. And when I was thirteen years old, so did my family.

As a teenager, I remember playing basketball at Druid Hill Park and learning that nobody called fouls. Hearing life lessons at the barbershop on Saratoga Street while the buzz of clippers shaped up my neck and sideburns. Scraping my knee while trying to show off for girls at Shake & Bake, a West Baltimore roller rink that protected kids inside it from the violence and neglect outside it. I didn't romanticize Baltimore. I knew that the city's problems paralleled much of the chaos I'd experienced in the Bronx—decaying infrastructure, failing schools, a drug epidemic that held the population in a vicious chokehold—but I still loved it. I spent my high school years in military school in Pennsylvania and joined the army right after high school. I graduated from junior college and then received my four-year degree back in Baltimore. During all those years, all those transitions, Baltimore was where I went back to when I was looking for a place to call home.

After college I left Baltimore again. I lived in Oxford, England, as a graduate student and in Afghanistan as a paratrooper in the US Army. I worked in Washington as a White House Fellow, and in New York as an investment banker.

Things were going well for me and my family—we lived com-
fortably in Manhattan. And then in 2013 I left finance to create a new organization to help bring college education to those
for whom it seems out of reach. My wife and I decided to pur-
sue those new dreams in my old hometown, Baltimore. Friends
in both New York and Baltimore questioned my decision. Was
my mom sick? Had I been fired? My answer was simple: I
wanted to come home.

As I sat in that Boston hotel room and watched my city descend into a state of emergency, I experienced a strange feeling. I felt guilty being away, but it wasn't just that. An audience
in Boston would listen to me talk about poverty, but at a historic moment in my own city's history, I was MIA. It felt symbolic of something deeper, and it troubled me.

I got home from my travels on Wednesday, April 29, almost
exactly forty-eight hours after the uprising kicked off. As I
drove through downtown, it was eerily quiet. National Guard
troops were deployed forty deep outside City Hall, which was
two blocks away from a police station, making it by far the saf-
est place in the entire city. I imagined what it must have been
like for those soldiers. I remembered wearing that same uniform: "full battle rattle," we called it. You join the Guard expecting to be called to address natural disasters such as floods
or hurricanes. Perhaps you'll be deployed to augment the
armed forces during times of war. But the other function of the
National Guard has been to serve as a patch for the unad-
dressed wounds of racial tension and economic disillusionment. Of the twelve times in our country's history that the
president of the United States has called in the National Guard,

only twice was racial conflict not involved: the 1970 postal workers' strike in New York and the looting after Hurricane Hugo on the island of St. Croix in the US Virgin Islands in 1989. The other occasions: the desegregation of a Little Rock schoolhouse in 1957, the integration of the University of Mississippi in 1962, the integration of the University of Alabama in 1963, the integration of Alabama schools in 1963, the Selma-to-Montgomery civil rights march in 1965, the Detroit riots of 1967, the riots in Chicago, Washington, and Baltimore after the murder of Martin Luther King Jr. in 1968, and the Los Angeles riots in 1992 after the Rodney King verdict.

The vast majority of the soldiers stationed near City Hall that day were not from Baltimore itself. For many, the only experience they'd previously had of Baltimore was going to see the Orioles play down at Camden Yards or maybe taking a field trip to the aquarium as a schoolkid. I remembered my own time as a soldier and what it was like patrolling areas that you were not familiar with. In Afghanistan, we patrolled communities that were understandably skeptical of us and our intentions. I tried to read and learn as much as I could about the spaces I was about to enter. But all the reading in the world didn't prepare me for what we faced, the burden of history reflected in the faces of the people we encountered. A history of foreigners arriving with conquest on their minds. A history of meeting those invaders with contempt, skepticism, fear, and resistance. And it was all justified. I walked into their neighborhoods loaded down with weapons and protective gear, a stranger from a distant land, and asked them to trust us, insisting we were there to help them. But the truth was that the people we encountered had rational reasons for their skepticism, and we'd been sent there to do an impossible job. I passed my brothers and sisters in uniform on the steps of City Hall and empathized as they stood watch over my brothers and sisters in our communities in Baltimore.

After stopping to check on my wife and kids, I went straight to church. At Bethel AME in West Baltimore, five minutes from where Freddie Gray had lived and died, a meeting was just starting, led by the church's pastor, Dr. Frank Reid. Dr. Reid has loomed large in my life since my return to Baltimore. Like many ministers in black communities, he does more than teach the Word: he advises, consoles, advocates, and inspires hope in communities where hope is not generously allocated. His grace and knowledge of not only God's word but earthly realities inspire me. We had spoken a few times over the previous few days, and he had asked me to stop by the church. When I got there, a hundred local pastors, gang leaders, and community members had gathered in Bethel's soaring sanctuary. Dr. Reid looked tired. You could probably count on the fingers of two hands the hours of sleep he had gotten over the past few days. He asked me to say a few words, and I stood self-consciously, still in sweatpants from the plane.

I told the gathering about something that had happened as I stood in a crowd at the airport watching CNN loop footage of buildings burning, knowing that this was happening in my own hometown. Suddenly a stranger near me, in khakis and a polo shirt, spat out: "Baltimore." I could tell from his scornful tone he wasn't from there.

I couldn't say I'd never complained about Baltimore; griping about your hometown can feel like a bit of a pastime. Baltimoreans have mastered it. We can spend hours in a bar or barbershop railing about how badly the city is doing. But then we pay our tab and head back to our homes and communities. Our tax dollars—and our abiding love for the place—pay for the right to complain about everything. But when outsiders complain, we take real issue with it.

Speaking to the crowd at Bethel, I tried to turn the stranger's contempt into a galvanizing moment, a rallying cry against apathy. When I was done, the assembled crowd merely clapped politely. Frustration and feelings of inadequacy overtook me again. When I looked out into the eyes of the people sitting in the pews, I realized why the response to my abbreviated speech had been so muted: many of the people there questioned what aspects of the city should be saved at all. On streets all around us, I knew, it was hard to tell which of the wrecked stores and rowhouses had been looted or burned that week and which had been falling apart for decades. Our meeting had to end within the hour, so that people could get home before the 10:00 P.M. citywide curfew that had been instituted the day after the National Guard showed up. Sitting with me in that sanctuary were street leaders who might be dead within the year. The life I was living and the future I dreamed about were unreachable for most of them.

This book is about more than Freddie Gray's death and its aftermath. This book is about more than Baltimore. It's about privilege, history, entitlement, greed, and pain. And complicity. Mine. All of ours.

Over the last few years I've returned to the story of those five days in Baltimore again and again, trying to understand the events at a human scale—what triggered the uprising, who was drawn into it on all sides, what motivated them. But it all started with questions that bubbled up in those first moments and have haunted me ever since: How much pain are we willing to tolerate in others? How much fear, death, and hopelessness will we accept when they fall on our neighbors? What can we learn from the people who throw themselves into the breach—those among us who stop looking away and give something, maybe even everything, to try to repair those gaps, to heal those wounds? And what do we learn from their failure?

Five Days will span the most dramatic period of the unrest, April 25–29, 2015. I spoke to people at all levels of the city's life, but seven lives stood out—an activist, a businessman, a cop, a basketball star turned rioter, a business manager and community protector, a fledgling politician, and a public defender. Their lives intersected at key moments, and taken together, their stories reveal a truer, fuller, and more surprising version of events and their context than what the media was able to show at the time. Their narratives tell a larger story about what happens when a city wakes to find the American dream is exactly that—an unconscious state that contains shades of reality but is ultimately unmoored from it. Woven together, their stories offer a true and kaleidoscopic vision of pain and redemption on the ground.

When my mind goes back to the day of Freddie Gray's funeral, I remember looking at his casket from the back of New Shiloh Baptist Church, Freddie's perfectly white shoes peeking out, pointing toward the heavens. My mind retreats to Nina Simone. Her rendition of the song "Baltimore" was as haunting in 2015 as it had been when she recorded it in 1978, the year of my birth. Nina Simone's torching voice entered over the distinctly reggae-drawn concoction of steel drums and bass guitars driving the steady, swaying beat. The melodic pulse was overpowered by the melancholy lyrics and unforgettable force of Nina Simone's roar. Listening to the song, you can imagine the high priestess of soul, eyes closed, gripping the microphone, singing her pain into a space that was occupied by too many.

Oh, Baltimore
Ain't it hard just to live
Just to live

Timeline: Before the Five Days

1989

Gloria Darden gives birth to twins, a boy and a girl. The twins are born two months premature. In her early twenties when she had the twins, Gloria had never attended high school. She could not read or write, and struggled with heroin addiction. Tiny and underweight, Freddie and his twin sister, Fredericka, spend their first months in the hospital. After five months, Gloria brings the twins back to the housing projects of West Baltimore.

1992

Freddie and his family move to 1459 N. Carey in West Baltimore. The home rents for $300 a month. In 2009, it and 480 homes just like it will be named in a civil suit regarding the endemic levels of lead paint throughout those houses. By age two, Freddie and his twin sister have elevated levels of lead in their blood and suffer lasting brain damage. The family lives on Carey Street until the twins are six years old.

1995

Freddie starts school at Matthew A. Henson Elementary School in Sandtown-Winchester. Because of the lead poisoning, Freddie's behavior poses considerable challenges to the school's teachers (statistically, among the least-experienced and worst-equipped educators in Baltimore City). His teachers enrolled Freddie in special education classes, which he would never leave. By the fifth grade, Freddie was four grade levels behind in reading. Driven out of the classroom by his intellectual disability, Freddie spends his early years in nearby recreation centers.

1998

Freddie is spending more and more time out of the classroom, experiencing increasingly long stretches out of school. Freddie starts to migrate to the corners and begins dealing drugs. At home, Freddie's stepfather leaves for drug rehab because of his heroin addiction. Without his income, Freddie's home experiences long stretches without electricity or running water. Freddie's godmother takes Freddie to church, where he volunteers delivering meals to senior citizens and washing cars.

2008

The Baltimore City Public Schools record Freddie's last attendance in school. He's eighteen. He's in the tenth grade.

2009

Freddie is arrested and sentenced to four years in prison for two counts of drug possession with intent to distribute.

2011

Freddie is paroled and back on the streets.

2013

Freddie is arrested again for drug possession and distribution. Shortly thereafter, Freddie's half brother, Raymond Lee Gordon, thirty-one years old, is gunned down near the Inner Harbor in downtown Baltimore.

APRIL 12, 2015

8:39 A.M.

At the intersection of W. North Avenue and N. Mount Street, four officers on bicycles attempt to stop Freddie Gray and another man who ran after making eye contact with the police.

8:40 A.M.

Police catch and arrest Freddie on the 1700 block of Presbury Street. According to police accounts, the arrest takes place without incident and no force is required.

8:42 A.M.

A police van is requested to take Freddie to the police station. At that point Freddie indicates he has asthma and asks for an inhaler. Minutes later when the van arrives, Freddie is put into leg irons and placed in the back of the van.

8:59 A.M.

At Druid Hill Avenue and Dolphin Street, the van driver requests a secondary unit to drive over and check on Freddie in the back of the van. Minutes later, the van Freddie is riding in is requested to go to 1600 North Avenue to pick up another recently arrested individual. There is some communication between the police officers and Freddie, and his behavior and physical condition seem off, enough so that the officers will later admit there was concern at that point that they "needed to assess Mr. Gray's condition, how we responded, were we able to act accordingly." After the stop, the van eventually continues to the Western District police station with both suspects.

9:26 A.M.

The city fire department responds to a call for paramedics to support an "unconscious male" at the Western District police station.

9:33 A.M.

The medics arrive and provide "patient care" for Freddie for twenty-one minutes.

9:54 A.M.

The medics depart with Freddie Gray for the Shock Trauma Center at the University of Maryland Medical Center.

APRIL 14, 2015

Freddie undergoes double surgery at Shock Trauma. It is determined that Freddie has three broken vertebrae and an injured voice box.

APRIL 15, 2015

Freddie remains in a coma.

APRIL 18, 2015

Word spreads about what happened to Freddie, and protests begin outside the Western District police station.

APRIL 19, 2015

At seven o'clock in the morning, Freddie is declared dead at Shock Trauma.

SATURDAY, APRIL 25

Tawanda

TAWANDA JONES HAD BEEN WAITING two years to join this march for justice. Well, not exactly *this* march—it was not for her brother but for another black man from the opposite side of town—but at the end of the day, she decided, any black man is every black man. Freddie Gray's death a week ago had breathed new life into the cases of others who had come before him, including Tawanda's brother, Tyrone West.

Two years on from her brother's death, Tawanda felt like everyone else had forgotten the one thing she knew she'd never get out of her mind: the July day his body had lain on the sidewalk, drenched in pepper spray from the violent arrest the police said he deserved.

There were two unreconcilable sides to the story: what the police said and what she knew in her heart. Their story: Her brother, a black man, large and hostile, had refused to follow orders and then struggled with them. They said that he was dehydrated and had a heart condition and died in the struggle. Her story: Her brother was murdered.

She had been screaming her story into microphones and

bullhorns every week for nearly one hundred weeks, in winter and summer, rain and sleet, armed only with posters of her gentle brother's face, his eyes pleading to the crowd to pay attention. For more than seven hundred days she had been taking her cause to the corners. Sometimes she was with whatever small group she could assemble—family, friends, occasionally strangers with gripes of their own. Sometimes she was alone, shouting into the Baltimore sky.

NO JUSTICE, NO PEACE.

ONE MAN, UNARMED.

JUSTICE FOR TYRONE WEST.

She called the protests "West Wednesdays." It had a ring to it. The news liked catchy slogans. And reporters from all the news outlets were going to be here today.

Tawanda had been asked by Freddie Gray's family to help lead the protest from Gilmor Homes, the housing project in West Baltimore where Freddie had been arrested, to City Hall. They knew about her commitment not just to her brother but also, beyond her own heartbreak, to the larger cause of addressing police violence and accountability. They respected her—the hours and days she'd already put into this work—and wanted her to stand with them. It was going to be the big protest to cap all the others that had sparked in the last week, ever since the news broke that the twenty-five-year-old would not survive the break in his spine.

She had watched all the shaky cellphone videos of Gray being dragged by the police, and Tawanda felt her soul pierced every time she heard his screams blare from the television—not just in sympathy for Gray but for herself, for she wished she had gotten to hear her brother's voice, even his screams, in his last seconds. But the videos were followed by a familiar script on the newscasts, one Tawanda recognized too well: *Black male. Encounter with police. Dead.*

Tawanda had met Freddie's mother, Gloria, at a protest exactly one week before the big march, while her son still lay in a coma at Shock Trauma. Tawanda was eager to give the Gray family something she had not been afforded after Tyrone's encounter with the police: hope.

"Don't give up hope," she told Freddie's mother. "He's going to pull through. I'm going to be praying for your son."

The following day, a Sunday, Freddie was pronounced dead.

When Tawanda heard the news, she was heartbroken, thinking over and over again about the moment the day before when she'd tried to console Freddie's mother, and for a moment Gloria had looked into her eyes with a flicker of hope. Tawanda decided then and there to dedicate the next West Wednesday, held outside the Western District Police Station, to Freddie.

There had never been any citywide marches for Tyrone. But after Freddie died, the protests persisted for days, and Tawanda watched as the city was roiled by protesters shouting the very thing she'd been screaming out every Wednesday for two years: that the Baltimore Police Department was the biggest gang in America, with a license to kill with impunity.

In the months and years prior to Freddie's death, young men with similar profiles had met similar fates. In 2012, Anthony Anderson was walking in his neighborhood on his way to his East Baltimore home when he was confronted by the police, who ordered him to stop moving. He "failed to respond" to commands and was tackled by a police officer. That tackle—or, as the Board of Estimates called it, a "bear-hug maneuver"—left Anthony Anderson's spleen ruptured and his ribs fractured. The internal bleeding killed him shortly after he arrived at the hospital. Initially investigators said Anderson died because he choked on drugs he was trying to hide from officers, but the medical examiner's report dismissed that claim, instead pinning the blame on Anthony's entire body weight slamming onto his neck and collarbone. The Anderson family was awarded $300,000 by the city of Baltimore. Even though the state medical examiner determined that he died by homicide, no officers were charged in his death.

Tyrone West had an altercation with law enforcement after a traffic stop in Northeast Baltimore. He was unarmed, and the state claimed his death was due to the heat of the day and a heart condition. Once again the city and state eventually dispensed of the matter through a civil settlement, paying Tyrone's three children $1 million. The details of these three cases were different, but they all have one crucial thing in common: despite the six- and seven-figure settlements, not a single officer was arrested, indicted, or found guilty of having any responsibility for the death of these unarmed African American boys and men.

The tension between law enforcement and the communities they were sworn to protect and serve had grown palpably thick in Baltimore. For many, the presence of police in the city's black neighborhoods brought not a sense of peace or security but its opposite. The sound of a siren strikes a different pitch depending on which neighborhood hears it. Still, after the investigations and payouts, most of the community found a way to go on with their lives. Till the next one.

Tawanda didn't go on with her life. For two years she held a lonely vigil demanding true accountability for her brother's death. But now everything she'd been saying was being amplified because of another death, and the world was watching. Maybe this time they would listen.

Still, though, all of the time she'd spent protesting, sometimes alone, had left her bruised. There had never been any marches for Tyrone. That still hurt, even as she looked for a good pair of shoes and prepared for the march of her life. She couldn't deny that part of her felt stung at seeing so many people in the city finally preparing for battle, but on behalf of someone else. For her brother, there had been only a handful of witnesses who seemed to care enough to speak up and speak out.

Of course, there were reasons Freddie's death was different, that it so quickly turned into a galvanizing moment instead of passing into painful silence like Tyrone's. Portions of Freddie Gray's final moments were caught on camera. Capturing video of police encounters is commonplace now, but Freddie's death in 2015 coincided with the emergence of smartphones and social media as tools of citizen journalism. None of those other victims of police violence had images of their final moments, their bodies laid out on the concrete, broadcast to a global audience. Footage of police killings was starting to show up on people's social media feeds raw, without being filtered through a controlled media narrative that adopted the police's point of view and implied that the victims "deserved it." Our generation would be the first to interact with violent death in this new way—through the same small window in our phones where we watched Eric Garner screaming "I can't breathe" while an officer straddled his back, yanking him to the ground like a steer, or a young Tamir Rice standing in a park as a squad car pulled up and an officer fired his weapon into the child, ending his life, or Walter Scott in Charleston, South

Carolina, being pulled over for a nonfunctioning brake light and soon after being shot in the back while fleeing, contradicting the officers' sworn testimony. Complaints about violent policing could no longer be treated as folklore or dismissed as exaggerations. "Our word versus yours" is less of a stalemate—where the tie goes to the state—when there is video evidence.

The other exceptional factor in Freddie's death was that it happened in the wake of so many other incidents between 2014 and 2016. The summer of 2015 was a bad one for police and community relations. According to *The Guardian*, in 2015 there were more than one hundred documented police killings of unarmed black people. All of these deaths were defended with different rationales and backstories, but the number is still staggering when you consider that each represents a case of an agent of the state using lethal violence against the accused—still innocent in the eyes of the law—who did not present an equal threat. Around that eighteen-month period alone, there was Mike Brown in Ferguson, Philando Castile in St. Paul, Laquan McDonald in Chicago, Alton Sterling in Baton Rouge. Each situation had its own particularities, but what they had in common was an obvious power imbalance that led to a death. In the aftermath of these killings, Freddie Gray's death was less a data point than a tipping point.

A movement arose to meet this moment. After the murder of Trayvon Martin in 2012, the Black Lives Matter movement was launched by Patrisse Khan-Cullors, Alicia Garza, and Opal Tometi, and their digital activism soon took on real-world form. By 2015, it was transitioning from a small group of disconnected activists to a global network with some forty chapters around the country, organized according to principles of distributed leadership and growing into a larger movement for black lives. By the time of Freddie's death there was an articulated framework for response and mobilization when police violence struck. The growing protests were not driven purely by emotion. Even if the system's response to Freddie's life was chaotic and unfocused, the response to his death was, at least at first, strategic and organized.

For two years prior, as Tawanda held her own protests, most acted as if she were crazy. Police, politicians, and passersby gave her sympathetic looks and offered comforting words to her face, but she knew that behind her back they were asking: "When is she going to stop doing this?"

She had an answer for that: never.

John

JOHN ANGELOS NEVER REALLY SAW himself going into the baseball business. After graduating from the Gilman School, arguably Baltimore's most prestigious independent preparatory school, and then Duke University, he went on to law school at the University of Baltimore, like his father, Peter. Law was the family business and his presumed career destiny. But in 1994, his father became the new owner of the hometown baseball franchise, the Baltimore Orioles, and wanted his sons, John and Louis, working in the business with him. Early on, John took on what he thought would be a temporary project. The Orioles were moving from seventy-five-year-old Memorial Stadium to a new park, Camden Yards, that would help anchor a rebuilt and reimagined downtown Baltimore.

Downtown Baltimore, bordered by its waterfront, used to be a collection of rat-filled docks where cargo ships came and went at a frenetic pace. Goods were traded, money was made. Not exactly a beauty at first glance, but there was a grace in its industriousness, a music in its cacophony of cultures and accents, foods and histories. Then, between 1958 and 1965,

Thomas D'Alesandro Jr., the thirty-ninth mayor of the city (and father of the eventual first female Speaker of the House, Nancy Pelosi), began the process of transforming the docks—a transformation that wasn't simply visionary but existentially vital, as shallow water levels and the growing size of container ships made reliance on shipping revenue foolhardy.

Mayor William Donald Schaefer first introduced an idea of an "Inner Harbor," where the now-dormant dockyards would be reborn as a social and shopping destination, like South Street Seaport in New York or the Historic District in Charleston, South Carolina. It would be a place where tourists and Marylanders alike could congregate and grab a good meal, walk along the waterfront, or catch a baseball or football game. Docks for container freights became plats for restaurants. Loading spaces became plazas. Sports would be the hub for other revenue-generating spokes. But the transition from homely and beloved Memorial Stadium, the open-air forge of memories for generations of Baltimoreans, to a freshly designed, newly built, trend-setting stadium was not simple. For one, Baltimore hated the idea.

Some detractors protested the amount of taxpayer dollars that had to go into the stadium—approximately $210 million—and how the congestion it generated would impact traffic on game days. Others pointed out that the city was dotted with neighborhoods that had been burned out decades ago and neglected for generations. These neighborhoods—both their buildings and the souls within them—were starved for attention and aid, yet when the Orioles and their wealthy owners needed a new stadium, the city jumped to pour millions into it. But public resistance wasn't the only obstacle. There was another challenge, seemingly trivial in comparison but incredibly important to those diehard Orioles fans lucky enough to care: *What will happen to my season ticket seats in the new stadium?* This was now John's problem.

John's job was to figure out a way to make the old *and* new season ticket holders happy. He would sit at the office until ten o'clock at night surrounded by charts and seat maps and stickers and lists of names, a mad scientist in his lab, studying patterns and designs only he could understand. This wasn't just about seats. It was about history and ego. Fairness and trade-offs. Art and math. And it was there that John fell in love with the work and its balance between operational details and the swirl of nostalgia, passion, legacy, and hope that defined fans' relationship to their home team. Most people who get into the business of sports aspire to go into player management, making personnel decisions: *Whom should we trade for? How much room do we have before we hit the luxury tax threshold? Is this player worth the money his agent is demanding?* John found his passion in a small room by himself, sitting with seating charts and equity holder equations, focusing on the fans, not the players. What started off as a one-off project turned into twenty years of his life.

When he moved up to the post of executive vice president in 1999, John used to receive updates during games from his deputy Neil Aloise on everything from attendance to rain delays to fans who had been ejected for bad behavior. Neil's comprehensive descriptions of every detail of what was going on in the ballpark impressed John. But now Neil was the head of ballpark operations, fully in charge of game-time issues. John hadn't seen Neil's name come up on his phone during a game in years, but on this Saturday afternoon in late April 2015 Neil called John around four o'clock, two and a half hours after the one-thirty first pitch—the game must be in its late innings, John thought.

"Hey, John, just want to keep you updated on some developments here."

Partee

MAJ. MARC PARTEE HADN'T EXPECTED his Saturday would go like this. It was supposed to be his day off, and he was looking forward to one of the two Saturdays a month he got to spend with his family. His son Marc Ahmal Partee was a seventeen-year-old powerlifter who looked like a younger version of his father, barrel-chested and thick, a presence so imposing you might miss the goofily disarming smile. That day he had a championship meet in Pennsylvania and his father had committed to cheering him on. His son had worked so hard for this.

That was the story he'd told his boss through gritted teeth the day before, when Lt. Col. Sean Miller had called and told him he'd have to work the following day. But there was no way Miller could accommodate him. "All hands on deck, more protests tomorrow," Miller told Partee. "Got to protect the jewel."

"The jewel" was the Inner Harbor. Its economic impact on Baltimore had become almost incalculable. Tourism alone represented over $700 million in revenue. The Inner Harbor was the city's post-industrial claim to fame, a shining diamond in a city known for its rougher edges.

And today Marc Partee's job was to protect the jewel. The first African American Inner Harbor police commander in history was about to be tested like never before. The thousands of protesters assembling that day planned to begin their march in West Baltimore, the largely impoverished neighborhood where Freddie Gray had lived and died, but then work their way to Partee's downtown jurisdiction. Gray's West Baltimore and the bustling Inner Harbor area could feel like different countries—the life expectancy in West Baltimore could be as much as twenty years shorter than in the Inner Harbor area, among other stark distinctions—but in truth they were only walking (or marching) distance apart. Protesters had announced that West Baltimore would be their staging area. They would start the march where Freddie had taken his last steps, then raise their voices in the precincts where Freddie's voice had never been heard.

Partee received more details in a subsequent call from his lieutenant. The protest route had already been mapped. Marchers would move from West Baltimore to City Hall, the focal point of the community's growing anger. They wanted the city's political leadership to hear their cries and feel their pain, their urgency. But the march wasn't just about feelings and catharsis: protesters wanted accountability and a promise that justice would be forthcoming. They would then take the march from the city's seat of political power to its center of commercial power, where tourists and well-heeled locals strolled the harbor and shopped, ate at outdoor cafes, and walked from their downtown hotels to the baseball stadium, where the Baltimore Orioles were set to play the Boston Red Sox in an evening game. It was an important early-season game between two competitive teams who might meet in the playoffs come fall. But Partee wasn't thinking about the playoffs. He was thinking that he was losing his Saturday to a city on the edge—and his dominion, "the jewel," was at the knifepoint.

Tawanda

THE MARCHES THROUGH THE STREETS of West Baltimore would be like those in the civil rights movement, the activist community said—not just a friendly protest but a confrontation, maybe a battle.

Tawanda wasn't worried. Once she had been shy and quiet. That was the Tawanda who'd been too scared to read a poem aloud in class as a child and who'd avoided conflict at all costs as an adult. But her brother's death had changed her. At some point over the last two years she'd become someone different. A warrior. She wasn't shaken by the possibility of confrontation. She would be front and center, locking arms, chanting, screaming, crying, demanding justice.

This was going to be the longest walk of her life, and she chuckled as she thought about how amused Tyrone would have been by the whole thing. He'd always been on her about staying fit and about the value of a good walk. He frequently walked from one side of the city to the other. But today the exact route didn't matter. She would be there to support Freddie Gray's family and walk with them.

The rallying point was West Baltimore, where Tawanda saw about three hundred people already assembled when she arrived. A mural of Freddie Gray by the street artist Nether would go up on the wall of an adjacent building about a week after the march, his lips in a half smile, and it almost felt like he was watching over the people, his modest beam offering appreciation and encouragement. The streets were full of people holding signs and holding each other. The music playing in the background served as a soundtrack, but she knew that this gathering was not celebratory. She was so proud of Freddie's mom, a steady force even in mourning. Heartbreaks like that can push people into one of two very different places: into public, to demand accountability and justice, or deeper into privacy, to grieve. It can feel like an impossible choice: whether to push for justice and progress or retreat to heal in silence. But it's the mothers, fathers, sisters, and brothers in the deepest throes of devastation who can hold the brightest flame for the dead, whose cry for justice has the greatest resonance and authority. And so they chose to march.

Gloria wore dark sunglasses, both to protect her eyes from the glare of the sun and to shield her from the national spotlight. Her low, sleepy eyes had seen so much in just over two decades, and the pain showed in her eyes. Tawanda wanted to be there for her and in a quiet way, maybe just through her presence, remind Gloria that to find justice she must persist. She wanted Gloria to find the strength to speak out, to see that momentum and attention were on her side and she couldn't take the chance of losing them. Freddie wouldn't want that. Neither would Tyrone.

At some point as the march wound its way through West Baltimore, Tawanda fell in alongside her cousin Qiara Butler. As the crowd started heading downtown the two cousins exchanged quizzical looks. Tawanda was informed that the plan was to head from Gilmor Homes to the Western District police station, and then to City Hall. That made sense to her. It followed the logic of her process for West Wednesdays: go to public but peaceful locations, and be transparent about your location and your reason for choosing it. But then Tawanda sensed a shift in direction. Wondering who was in charge, Tawanda looked to her right at Malik Zulu Shabazz, former leader of the New Black Panthers and co-founder of Black Lawyers for Justice. He yelled to the crowd that although they were supposed to be going to City Hall, they should head to the Inner Harbor, telling the protesters, "Let's hit them where their pockets are."

Tawanda was nervous about going downtown, because she didn't like trouble. She also knew that when you go off target, you become vulnerable. And bringing this crowd of protesters—their emotions increasingly inflamed as they moved closer to Baltimore's power center—felt like trouble.

When the Gray family looked confused about the change in direction, Tawanda's anxiety increased. The family had told her that Shabazz was there as support, since he had experience leading rallies all over the country, but when Tawanda saw Shabazz's steely focus, she began to understand that his idea of support might have been different from hers. But Tawanda wanted to respect Freddie's family and be there for them. So she followed their lead, following Shabazz.

The hours of "No justice, no peace," and the call-and-response chants of "What do we want? Justice! When do we want it? Now!" began to fade as the crowd readied to move past City Hall. Around 4:00 P.M., Shabazz looked back with an ornery smirk at a *Baltimore Sun* reporter and said, "Let's shake it up at this baseball game." Another reporter asked him where the crowd was going and he responded, "I don't know, to shut something down." With his bullhorn, he steered the large crowd of increasingly angry protesters toward downtown. Tawanda's premonitions of trouble grew stronger.

As they moved closer to the Inner Harbor area, they were confronted with scores of police officers, a human barricade blocking the streets leading to the harbor. Protesters were being funneled toward the baseball stadium and the adjacent M&T Bank Stadium, where the Baltimore Ravens played American football. The stadiums were situated only a few hundred yards from each other, a choice intended to consolidate commerce around the stadiums, but one that also created a natural pattern for foot traffic. And as the protesters surged toward the stadium, the control of the message got looser.

News cameras were following the march, and Tawanda was determined to get in front of as many as possible. She thought it was important that the message that went out to the public was a disciplined one.

"One man, unarmed," she said over and over again, her mind on Tyrone and so many others.

She was being interviewed by a CNN reporter when the second big story of the day began to emerge.

Tawanda noticed as they got closer to Camden Yards that there was an Orioles game today—she could tell from the number of alcohol-fuelled fans wandering around and the larger-than-usual crowds, who used the occasion of an Orioles game and a clear spring day to hang around the stadium and enjoy a meal. Many of these folks were clearly from the suburbs and probably oblivious that their casual outing in the city coincided with protests for a twenty-five-year-old black man who had lost his life in police custody. Tawanda was there for justice, and in no mood for foolishness—particularly foolishness spurred by outsiders. But just as dusk started to settle, foolishness arrived.

The marchers became more agitated as they filtered through the downtown streets at sunset. When they walked past the glittering windows of the Gallery, a shopping mall, Tawanda noticed a white protester just behind her flip a trash can. As the metal container bounced against the asphalt, spilling out its contents, the man yelled, "This is for Freddie!" Before Tawanda could respond, a member of Freddie's family quickly moved toward the sandy-haired man, yelling, "Uh-uh, we ain't doing that. We want peace." Surrounding protesters moved in around the man, seemingly to reinforce the wishes of the family, and the man sheepishly apologized and tried to blend back into the crowd. But Tawanda worried that this march had the potential to get out of hand, and fast. The crowd was large. Many of the faces she could see were unfamiliar, and some of the people around her had covered their faces with T-shirts or masks. She looked back over at her cousin, whose expression was starting to reveal some tension. She squeezed Freddie's mom's hand a little tighter.

"We want all six," the crowd was chanting now as they made their way through the streets leading to Camden Yards. The "six" they were referring to were the six officers who had arrested Freddie Gray.

The peaceful march Tawanda had volunteered to help lead was clearly morphing into something else, something chaotic—the energy was getting more violent. Tawanda could feel the short fuse of the protest burning its way toward something explosive.

Suddenly her attention was drawn to a commotion nearby.

She watched as a white man with a beer bottle in his hand wandered into the crowd.

"Screw Freddie Gray," he said. "He was a thug."

"What you say?" voices from a group of black protesters roared back. Some of them started making their way toward the bars on either side of the street. Tawanda could feel a growing fury in the air now, and some of the protesters were looking for a place to unload it. The opportunity presented itself when the white man threw his bottle into the crowd of black protesters and the police stood and did nothing.

Next thing she knew, black and white arms began to swing in the air.

She stood frozen in disbelief as the situation escalated fiercely and quickly. Soon after, she saw young men standing on top of police cars, jumping on the hoods and striking the windows and windshields until they shattered.

Tawanda was shocked at how quickly everything had turned. She knew they shouldn't have come downtown. It felt almost unreal when she saw the police showing up on horses; never in her life had she seen police officers roll up on those before. *Good thing they have horses*, she thought, *because every police car in sight is probably damaged.*

Partee

UNDER NORMAL CIRCUMSTANCES, PARTEE'S NEARLY twenty years on the job as a Baltimore police officer would have bought him some sway to push back on having to come in on his day off, all the way from his home in Delta, Pennsylvania. Delta is a small town right on the border with Maryland and has a population of less than a thousand people. His home was large and had a lawn, a taste of middle-class life he didn't think he could have in the city. But it wasn't just the quiet and spaciousness of Delta he liked; it was also the distance. He felt far away from the streets of Baltimore when he was home, away from the stresses of his job. That was something he had in common with many of his colleagues—he was one of the more than 80 percent of Baltimore City police officers who didn't live in the city proper.

But Partee had been born at Baltimore's University Hospital and raised on the city's west side. The west side of Baltimore has a reputation for being neglected and depressed, but Partee knew that as soon as you passed Pimlico you were fine. He grew up in a big house on Woodland Avenue, a single-family home big enough that he and his two siblings could all have their own rooms. His grandparents lived next door and helped raise him. Partee's grandfather in particular cast an imposing shadow over his childhood. Partee modeled himself on his grandfather, who instead of finishing high school had decided to drop out and make a career in the Marines. Partee both feared and idolized his grandfather, the family patriarch and usually the only man around. Partee's own father lived around the corner, but they never really saw each other. His father was a big man, like Partee would grow up to be, and his large Afro only made his impressive frame all the more imposing. He worked at Pat Hayes Buick. Partee's mother never said anything bad about him to her son, but she didn't have to. He made an early habit of setting up times to meet his son and then standing Partee up. It happened so many times that eventually Partee stopped bothering to make appointments—why schedule rejection?

Partee attended one of the city's premier academic schools, the selective and historic Baltimore City College high school, known as "City," and nicknamed "Castle on the Hill" for its hilltop location and reputation for educating some of the city's greatest civic leaders since its founding in the nineteenth century. Partee still wears his class ring from 1992–93, the year City's football team went undefeated. He was a star on that team and was offered full scholarships out of high school to Morgan State University and Loyola University, two schools that were right in Baltimore, but he decided instead to go to Morehouse College in Atlanta, one of the oldest historically black colleges in the country. He loved the picturesque, all-male liberal arts college, whose alumni ranged from Dr. King to Spike Lee, but Morehouse wasn't cheap. After two years, he transferred back home to Morgan State, where he could complete his education on scholarship. He was a proud Baltimorean, but he wanted to explore the country; he thought maybe after Morgan he would try to find work somewhere else, forge his future somewhere else. That had been over two decades ago. He'd only gotten as far as Delta. Forty-nine miles from where he was born.

Partee thought about his father. His father had never seen him play football or any other sports, had never seen him win a tournament or a championship. Partee was not just at his son's tournament because he loved watching Marc participate in a sport he was passionate about. He came to watch his son because, in his mind, that's what men do. That's what real fathers do. It was Partee's greatest joy to be the father his own father hadn't been. That's why his Saturdays off meant so much to him, and why it pained him to consider how the rest of his day would look. He would need to leave soon if he was going to make it to Baltimore to be on time. He watched as young Marc triumphed in another round of the tournament. His precisely trimmed mustache curved around the edges of his mouth as he beamed toward his oldest child.

Now it was time to head back to Baltimore. It was time to protect the jewel.

John

A T DINNER EARLIER IN THE evening, his phone had buzzed about every ten minutes with fresh text updates from Neil: the protesters were heading toward Camden Yards, the protesters had surrounded the stadium, the chorus of protests outside of the ballpark had begun to drown out fans inside. When John's phone finally rang, he knew things must have escalated even more dramatically, because Neil never called unless it was urgent.

"The police said they want to keep the fans inside," Neil said.

John was nervous about the idea of trapping fans—some of them already slightly intoxicated—inside the stadium after the game was over. But a perimeter of protesters had formed at one of the main entrances, the North Gate (at the south end of Eutaw Street), and words and fists had already been exchanged with fans trying to leave early. John weighed the risk for the fans. What was worse, locking them in or turning them out to face the protesters?

John had never had to deal with anything like this before.

Fans acting up inside the stadium, even fighting, is an every-day occurrence in major league ballparks, but conflict between those on the inside and outside was something new. To John, though, it felt terribly symbolic.

John knew that people come to baseball games to get away from the real world. Fandom is an escapist journey, the sports arena the palace where the struggles of politics, your job, or your community don't matter. As long as the O's were win-ning, the hot dogs and beer were plentiful, and the Oriole Bird, the team's mascot, skipped around the stands posing with lit-tle children and making parents smile, all was right with the world. Fans don't want controversy and volatility, at least not when they're at the game. John believed that this was the prob-lem people have with actors making political speeches at the Academy Awards, or athletes doing so at the ESPYs, or foot-ball players kneeling during the anthem. That's not what peo-ple want from professionals who are supposed to entertain them. Years later, there would be a controversy when Laura Ingraham, a bombastic flamethrower on Fox News, finished a rant about politics in sports by telling LeBron James to "shut up and dribble." Ingraham's rant was laced with racist subtext and intentional provocation, but the truth is her feelings on the matter are not exceptional—lots of people believe the job of athletes and entertainers is to share their talents with fans, not their opinions about the real world.

But John had begun to notice how the political and stereo-typical crept into sports conversation. White players are "scrappy and smart," black players are "athletically gifted." Fans come to NFL games to see women and men in their gen-dered roles of sexually objectified cheerleaders and warrior players. The US military pays the NFL millions of dollars each year for military tributes during games, when jets fly overhead and attendees are asked to stand as the troops are honored—as if the gladiator pit were an adjunct to the military-industrial complex. Members of the Angelos family, the team's "owners," are referred to as "Mr. Angelos," as if this were a company town and they are the rightful bosses of us all, but the players are often referred to by first names or even nicknames. If sports fandom has a politics, it's decidedly conservative—not in terms of policies but in the sense that professional sports frequently affirms narrow, retrograde ideas of patriotism, gender roles, capitalism, and race. John didn't think of himself as a conservative, far from it, but he prized his role as the fans' advocate. He wanted to understand the problems of the world around him and the ways they infiltrated the world of sports—but he didn't want to remind the fans of it. It was what made his role increasingly fraught, at least in his mind. And now for the first time since joining the team, he was forced to wrestle with the messy, jagged reality of the world outside converging in a very literal way with the fantasy of escape that fans were expecting to find inside the stadium. This tension was always there to some extent; it was what made the fantasy so powerful. Now, though, not only could the organization not mask the tension and sell only the escape, it was at the epicenter of the collision between fantasy and reality. John didn't have all the details yet, but he did have a feeling that something had hit a breaking point, that something was changing. And Camden Yards was at ground zero.

Partee

"INCIDENT COMMAND, THIS IS 600! Permission to engage! Incident Command, they are busting through the windows, permission to engage!" Partee was screaming into his police radio and then cursing the silence that he heard in response. "Incident Command" was the call sign for his leaders, the brass who were moving the pieces on a chessboard that was on fire. Every one of the district commanders had a unique call sign, so the commanders knew whom they were speaking to. Central District was 100, Northern was 500. As the head of the Northwest District, Partee was 600. As he screamed into the radio he felt 600 was also his priority order. He had been trying to get positive engagement orders from his commanders for the past five minutes. A group of young men were kicking the windows of the Michael Kors store across the street from the Inner Harbor. This was far from the only incident within his area of operations, but this one was just ten yards from where Partee stood in his police blues. He was not wearing riot gear; when he'd showed up at his post at two-fifteen that afternoon, he was not expecting to need it, since none of the prior protests over the past few days had required it. He hadn't been warned this one would be so different.

Partee's unit was officially called the Inner Harbor Unit, but some in the community called them "the Bumblebees" because of the checkered patches on their uniforms and the way they seemed to swarm at the first sign of trouble. The patches were a celebration of the Baltimore flag, a patchwork of black and old gold with Baltimore's Battle Monument anchoring the center. The monument had been built to commemorate the soldiers who fought against the British in the War of 1812.

The Inner Harbor Unit was certainly prepared for protests, but that didn't mean they were prepared for riots. Partee had seen protests before. Groups of protesters would stand at City Hall shouting catchy slogans and rallying cries. Emotions might run high, but eventually everything would calm down and the crowd would disperse. The protests following the death of Freddie Gray had been more emotional and intense than usual, maybe, but not sustained, and until today hadn't escalated beyond slogans.

Partee's contingent of officers included six platoons, each with about twenty-three officers, as well as officers from Montgomery County and Prince George's County who'd come to help in anticipation of increased protest intensity. Montgomery and Prince George's Counties are relatively affluent neighbors to Baltimore, but they also bump up against Washington, DC. Many officers who start their careers in Baltimore City migrate to these other counties for the higher pay and easier conditions. As one officer said, "More pay, less drama, easy decision."

A little more than an hour after he arrived, Partee noticed marchers coming down Pratt Street, a major thoroughfare that hugs the Inner Harbor. He began placing his people in position to detour protesters. He knew he had to funnel them in another direction in order to keep their focus off the economic fulcrum of the city. He lined up his officers in front of one of the major entry points to the promenade, and had the rest line up in front of the harborside shops. As the marchers followed the commands of Shabazz and groups started moving toward the eastern side of the promenade, he set up a line on the backside of the Light Street pavilion, so if the protesters made it to the Harbor, they'd be surrounded: on one side they would face Baltimore City police officers, on the other side would be the water. Partee's strategy took him back to his earliest lesson at the police academy: use the terrain as your ally. As he'd soon learn, that hard lesson could cut both ways.

John

JOHN ANGELOS SAT IN THE passenger seat of his white Jeep Grand Cherokee, typing feverishly into his phone. Getting updates. Giving feedback. Margaret, to whom he'd been married for over a decade, was in the driver's seat, her eyes focused on the New York Thruway. They were on vacation and on their way to their second home in Saratoga Springs, New York. But his mind was on his first home. Three hundred and sixty miles south.

John's father, Peter Angelos, had been raised in Baltimore by Greek immigrant parents. They lived in Patterson Park, a working-class neighborhood, and his parents, John and Frances, stressed education and mobility for their family. Their son took those lessons very seriously. He graduated at the top of his class in high school, and eventually went to college and law school at the University of Baltimore; the law school's main administrative building now bears his family name. He tried his hand in politics, becoming the first Greek American elected to the Baltimore City Council, and in 1967 he made Maryland history when he was the first candidate for Baltimore City mayor ever to run on an interracial ticket. He lost with only 10 percent of the vote, and his advocacy for social justice took a different form when he left politics behind for law and business—he started a firm that eventually became one of the largest and most powerful law firms in the state for personal injury, medical malpractice, and class action suits. His success in the business world made his sphere of influence even greater than it would have been if he'd managed to get elected mayor all those years ago. He dined with senators and vice presidents. He had ambassadors and congresspeople on speed dial.

In 1993, the owner of the Baltimore Orioles, venture capitalist Eli Jacobs, went into bankruptcy and was forced to put the team up for auction. Judge Cornelius Blackshear led an auction that lasted just a minute, but finished with the price of the team at a record $173 million, over $100 million more than the previous owner had paid for it. Baltimore cheered when Angelos purchased the team—this was a homeboy, not a New York financier or California real estate developer. When asked if he could make money on the team after buying it for such an exorbitant price, his answer was, "That's not the primary concern. The primary concern is putting the best club on the field." Again Baltimore cheered. This owner, no matter how rich, was one of their own.

Now the 2015 baseball season was under way, and Baltimore's team of bright young stars was a fun group to watch—they enjoyed playing the game and, importantly, they liked each other. They were representing a city that took its sports, and its sports legends, very seriously. Baltimore is a city where people can tell you where they were when Orioles infielder Cal Ripken Jr. broke the record for consecutive games played, with his 2,131st game. It is a town that can tell you their vivid memories of waking up on March 29, 1984, to learn that the night before, the Baltimore Colts had packed up and moved the franchise to Indianapolis, leaving the city with a bitter void for twelve years before the Ravens finally made their debut. It's a city that prides itself on names like Johnny Unitas and Brooks Robinson, Jim Palmer and Ray Lewis, Earl Weaver and Brian Billick, names and eras the city could look back on with pride and hope.

Partee

"**I**NCIDENT COMMAND, THIS IS 600! Jesus, please respond. Permission to engage!"

There were commands coming over the police radio fast and furious, constant chatter and directives—but none responding to Partee. All of the radio traffic was about some kind of commotion taking place at the stadium, and officers were rapidly being reassigned to Camden Yards. When Partee's day had begun he'd had multiple platoons at his disposal, as well as neighboring jurisdictional police forces. He was now down to one platoon. Twenty-three officers to cover the entire Inner Harbor. Partee was a victim of his own success: he'd done such a good job of funneling protesters away from the Inner Harbor that a large cohort of them were now heading toward the stadium. In a rather ironic turn of events, Partee found himself covering his area of operations with a small fraction of his usual force because his officers had been redeployed to deal with a fresh challenge Partee himself had helped to create.

Partee ran back and forth from one side of the harbor to the other, moving his handful of officers around in an attempt to make it seem like there were more law enforcement officers protecting the Inner Harbor than there actually were. His hulking frame darted between line officers, many only a few years older than his son. He remembered his riot training: *In the chaos of a riot, anyone can be a target. People will be prey. Civilians. Officers. Schoolkids. Dope boys. Churchgoers. Soft targets are easier to hit. Be a hard target. People think twice about going after hard targets.* He knew that in the fever of the protest just the sight of his officers in uniform triggered anger. His blue uniform drenched in sweat, an exhausted Partee ran around telling his officers to move. *Change positions. Don't be seen in the same place twice.*

He had seen disturbances in Baltimore before. He'd been an officer for two decades; how could he not have? Localized skirmishes triggered by localized frustrations. Kids on one block riled up and looking for confrontation over some specific, if sometimes obscure, conflict. It was why he felt frustrated with the phrase "black-on-black crime." People committed crimes against the people they were closest to—it was no more complex than proximity and no more interesting.

Usually when police engage, youthful courage dissipates and people scatter. But today was different. Young men were now smashing windows knowing the police were staring right at them. People were using random objects they found on the street, with chairs from outdoor cafes or the orange street cones used to direct movement becoming projectiles. He could make out faces in the crowd—some sagging with disgust and disillusionment, some tightening with mournful rage, some flashing with opportunism, some fixed on action. They were angry. He watched as the protests started disaggregating: the marchers who were chanting in unison and the kind who had brought their children with them began to separate from the other, more aggressive protesters who had become heat-seeking missiles looking for direct contact.

This wasn't like other marches he'd seen, Partee thought. Something had changed after Freddie Gray's death. The young people knew the police were under increased scrutiny. They knew the news media were all over, hoping to catch that award-winning photo of overly aggressive policing. There was an unprecedented boldness.

Standing at the main promenade, an open area usually used for street performances against the backdrop of large ships, Partee picked up his taser and pointed it at the young men now approaching his line. He didn't have any intention of shooting them, but the taser projected a red laser beam that landed as a dot on its target, similar to the red dot that a sniper's scope sends out before the sniper turns someone into a fresh kill. He did it for effect: he wanted the men to experience the fear of seeing that dot appear on their own skin, the fear of standing next to someone when that dot appears on them. He wanted the fear to snap them out of their frenzy.

One of the young men noticed the dot and took it to mean that the Baltimore Police Department was about to gun them all down. He yelled out, and he and the others fled. They ran up Calvert Street, a broad north–south street that took them away from the Inner Harbor and out of Partee's jurisdiction. It was legal for Partee to use his scope light that day—although laws would later change—but he wasn't concerned with legality. He wanted to stop those young men, and he did. He just wanted the day to end. He was frustrated by the seeming anarchy and law enforcement's inability to quell it. And he was tired of shouting into a police radio and getting nothing back.

Tawanda

T AWANDA STOOD IN THE MIDDLE of the scattered and confused remnants of what had once been an organized
march. As the police presence increased, so did the anger and
frustration of the marchers. Young men were still jumping on
police cars, and Tawanda could hear them start to yell out
names with every kick.

"This for my Uncle Black that got killed by you bastards."

"This is for beating that man."

"This is for when you jacked me up and called me a bitch in
front of my girlfriend and you spit in my face."

Tawanda listened as these boys, children as young as ten
and no man older than twenty-five, told a story—the story of
what had happened before Freddie, before Tyrone, before the
marches. A US Department of Justice report would spell it all
out in a couple of years—these were the kids whose mothers
were molested by police officers, were called "bitches" and
"tricks," and were propositioned for sex. Whose fathers were
humiliatingly stopped and frisked for no reason. These were

the kids who were next in line to be debased and devalued, winding up behind bars or in the ground.

Tawanda felt like something powerful and suppressed was being unleashed. Today the kids were fighting back. And it frightened her.

The last time she'd been this scared was when she was twelve, when she and her friends were attacked by a group of skinheads while walking home from school. The men were all wearing T-shirts, and many were tattooed—one had a swastika inked on the side of his head, his loyalty branded on his skin. The men started screaming at her and her friends and then moved in closer and started kicking them. When Tawanda and her friends ran, the skinheads chased them down the street, waving baseball bats and calling them niggers. It was complete chaos, and Tawanda was petrified. She and her friends ran all the way back to the school, where they banged on the locked door, hoping to find some sanctuary from the attack. The school's white principal would not let them in. The youngsters were screaming and crying, pleading to be let in. The principal saw the men with bats coming. Still he told them, "You can't come in this door."

Tawanda and her friends hid behind some bushes, and when they saw a chance, they ran out and sprinted up Falls Road. Eventually she and her friends took refuge in a laundromat. But the white woman who worked there wanted them out. When Tawanda and her friends locked themselves in and refused to leave, the woman threatened to call the police. Tawanda remembered an overwhelming sense of relief at the threat—a call to the police was just what they needed to save them. How things had changed.

Tawanda's memories were interrupted by her phone buzzing. It was her fiancé, telling her that things were starting to get violent—it was no longer just a few windows getting smashed, and people were now starting to put their hands on each other—and he told her to get out of there. Tawanda realized that her car and her cousin's car were still in West Baltimore, where things had seemed so promising just a few hours ago. She and Qiara began running away from the crowd and called a family member to pick them up. She and seven other people piled themselves into the small silver coupe, some sitting on the others' laps, crowded and uncomfortable, but desperate to get out.

As they sped away down Light Street, away from the chaos, Tawanda saw that someone had thrown a trash can through the window of the Michael Kors store.

John

JOHN WAS STRESSED OVER THE idea of keeping the crowd in the stadium, which he thought was a bad idea, but he also recognized that the police had the final say. At an average Orioles game there would be forty-four officers from the Baltimore Police Department, and the Maryland Stadium Authority provided some private security people as well, numbering about thirty. The Orioles also hired events staff, about a hundred of whom are security. Add to those the plainclothes "fans" who are really security personnel, and the stadium is typically sufficiently secured. John was going over the numbers in his head when he felt the buzz of his phone again. Neil's normally excited voice took on a mild timbre, the way doctors are trained to share bad news.

"They made the call—they are keeping them in."

Minutes later Neil reported to him it was done. The public address announcer had asked for everyone's attention. The scoreboard lit up with the same script the PA announcer read from: *Due to an ongoing public safety issue, the mayor of Baltimore*

City and the Baltimore City police department have asked all fans to
remain inside the ballpark until further notice. Thank you.

John felt desperate for more information. Usually he attended home games to feel the pulse of the fans. He prided
himself on that. Now he was worried that the calm of Neil's
voice did not fully capture what was going on in the stadium.
Looking for direct, unfiltered feedback, he turned to Twitter.

He did not have a large Twitter following or follow very
many people himself; mainly he used Twitter to look at trending hashtags and zone out. He certainly didn't tweet himself.
John was always cautious of saying too much. One reason was
that he knew he couldn't just speak for himself; because of his
position and his last name, he represented an organization and
a legacy. He also didn't think people cared very much about
what he thought. His wife always told him he should speak up
more and use his voice.

Margaret was much like her husband in that both were
strikingly attractive and disarming. Margaret had grown up
in a working-class home, though often without the "working"
part. Unemployment and economic uncertainty had been the
norm, and music had always been her release. A singer and
songwriter, she had a talent for telling sometimes traumatic
real-life stories to a rhythm that people could dance to. It was
also how she'd met John fifteen years earlier, in a bar in her
hometown of Saratoga Springs. She knew John had plenty of
opinions about Baltimore and the way it so violently cleaved
along class and race lines.

John was well aware of how absurdly lucky and privileged
he was. It troubled him deeply that an accident of birth had set
him on such a radically different trajectory than others born
in the same city, even in the same hospital. He wasn't really

political. In fact, he hated politics, precisely because it so often failed to address these divides—it couldn't even address the fear so many Baltimore families had of the police force that was supposed to be there to help them.

John had first heard about Freddie Gray a couple of weeks ago, the same way as most of Baltimore—through the local news incessantly running stories about the young man who'd fallen into a coma after he was arrested by Baltimore PD. He was familiar with the increasingly unavoidable images of Freddie in his black shirt and blue jeans being dragged to the white police transport van; of Freddie's screams being met by officers demanding that he walk; his legs refusing or unable to comply, and two officers carrying all of his 160 pounds into the back of the vehicle. John couldn't imagine what it must have been like for Freddie in those moments. He also knew he would never have to.

John understood that his father's success had dramatically altered the destiny of future generations in their family, and he also knew that his father had made his fortune at a time and place where his ambitions and luck met a society that structurally supported his wealth creation. John grew up in a family with activist leanings, and he'd been raised to always challenge the system to bend toward equity and inclusion. But then again, that was the same system that allowed his family to thrive—a system where government funds, local and national policies, the actions of the police, and other factors calcified that luck into permanent advantage. John felt the tension in occupying that space.

As Margaret drove he searched for the hashtag #orioles on Twitter. As expected, he saw a wide variety of emotional comments, not about the game but about the fact that fans in the stadium were not being allowed to leave. People expressed confusion, fear, anger, frustration.

One series of tweets in particular caught his attention. Brett Hollander is a popular local radio host in Baltimore. His main beat is anything Baltimore: crabbing, local elections, whatever the new exhibit is at the Baltimore Museum of Art. He is good at his job, which means never being afraid to share his opinion. And with tens of thousands of followers, his influence in the larger Baltimore metro area was real. One of his followers was John Angelos.

They had never met before. They were not friends. But when John read Hollander's message that day, he felt that the radio host's comments struck right at the heart of his own dilemma. Hollander had written:

Everyone should feel fortunate for our freedoms in this country, as written in our Constitution. . . . I'm by no means a legal scholar, so please understand that, but protests should not violate the basic freedoms of non-protestors. People of a community should be able to commute, commerce should happen & citizens who want to go to a ballgame should be able to go. And any really important message out of these protests is lost when the rest of the community is disrupted.

John read the tweets aloud in the car. Margaret listened thoughtfully.

"You have to say something," she said. "I can't be the only one listening to you complain."

John opened the notes app on his cellphone and began typing. John's thumbs danced along his phone screen. He typed, deleted, paused, and then repeated the same cycle. He wanted to be careful with what he said. He knew he was a private citizen who was entitled to his own thoughts, but he'd always known the power his name held. First he attempted to express his feelings in 140 characters, the length limit of a tweet at the time. When he realized that would be impossible, he finally decided to just type it all out and break everything up into a thread of tweets. He told Margaret he didn't think his tweets would make a difference, but she replied, "Well, I guess we're going to find out if your theory is right," knowing he would take it as a challenge.

A little after nine o'clock, he hit send. The son of the owner of the Orioles, the chief operating officer of the team, was now entering the fray.

Brett speaking only for myself i agree with your point that the principle of peaceful, non-violent protest and the observance of the rule of law is of utmost importance in any society. MLK, Gandhi, Mandela, and all great opposition leaders throughout history have always preached this precept. Further, it is critical that in any democracy investigation must be completed and due process must be honored before any government or police members are judged responsible.

That said, my greater source of personal concern, outrage and sympathy beyond this particular case is focused neither upon one night's property damage nor upon the acts but is focused rather upon the past four-decade period during which an American political elite have shipped middle class and working class jobs away from Baltimore and cities and towns around the US to 3rd world dictatorships like China and others plunged tens of millions of

good hard working americans into economic devastation
and then followed that action around the nation by dimin-
ishing every American's civil rights protections in order to
control an unfairly impoverished population living under an
ever-declining standard of living and suffering at the butt
end of an ever-more militarized and aggressive surveillance state.

The innocent working families of all backgrounds
whose lives and dreams have been cut short by excessive
violence, surveillance, and other abuses of the bill of
rights by government pay the true price, an ultimate price,
and one that far exceeds the importance of any kids'
game played tonight, or ever, at Camden Yards. We need
to keep in mind people are suffering and dying around the
US and while we are thankful no one was injured at Camden Yards, there is a far bigger picture for poor Americans
in Baltimore and everywhere who don't have jobs and are
losing economic civil and legal rights and this makes inconvenience at a ball game irrelevant in light of the need-
less suffering government is inflicting upon ordinary
Americans.

As soon as they got back to the house in Saratoga Springs,
only an hour after he'd sent his first message, Margaret called
out to John, "Babe, you are a trending topic on Facebook."
John checked his Twitter account, wanting to see what people
were saying, wondering whether or not they agreed with
him—and curious about how much trouble he had gotten himself into. His eyes widened as he realized he was now trending
nationally.

Margaret looked at him and said, "Guess I was right. People
do care."

SUNDAY, APRIL 26

Greg

GREG BUTLER HAD TO GET back to Baltimore. He had been looking forward to his trip to Virginia Beach—chase some girls, blow off some steam. He'd even gotten a fresh haircut. Instead, he found himself sitting in his hotel room, eyes fixed on the television screen, where CNN was showing images of Baltimore erupting in violence.

It hadn't been much of a vacation. The troubles of home had followed him to Virginia, anyway: a boy had been shot and killed in Virginia Beach the day he'd arrived, and the town was buzzing about it all day Saturday. Though Greg didn't know him, he felt connected, maybe even responsible—that somehow he'd brought a bad omen with him. Because for the past forty-eight hours, Greg had felt death stalking him.

It started with Ms. Joyce—he called her "J.P.," like everyone she loved did. She had died on Friday. He'd always thought she was invincible, and her death devastated him.

Ms. Joyce had always been so proud of him. He could tell from the sparkle in her eye when she saw him show up at her door to do home improvement projects.

Her house was bedecked in art from her travels throughout Africa, and her bookshelves were lined with the works of great black authors. To visit her was to take a trip into a curated exhibit of the black experience. She always asked about his life and basketball. She never reprimanded him for doing what many young men did—wearing his pants low, smoking weed, chasing after girls. She never judged him.

When she died, she was seventy-something but youthful. She'd lived a modest life, yet she'd always carried herself like a woman of the world. She was everything Greg wanted to be: educated, unapologetically black, and respected for it. She'd been fighting cancer for months and was convinced that the holistic medicines she took would cure her. Greg believed she would pull through, because she always did. But then she didn't. And Greg was reminded that the world doesn't reward goodness or struggle.

When he'd heard the next day about the young man killed in Virginia Beach, it felt like dark forces were taking over.

Kareem was the final blow. Greg got word on Sunday that the thirty-six-year-old had been killed just before midnight Saturday. The father of Greg's childhood friend John, Kareem was a beloved and complicated man in both life and death. He was shot in what seemed a well-executed setup—or at least that's the only way that the neighborhood could make sense of the shooting of a man with so much power, money, charisma, and protection.

Kareem had been revered in the streets, and he'd cultivated a strong sense of hood loyalty. He was his own boss. He made enough money to move his kids out of the hood, make sure their wardrobes were set, send them to better schools, make sure they had a safe neighborhood to play in. He was still re-spected enough to draw a crowd when he ventured back to his old block on business. But on the other side of town from where masses had gathered hours earlier to protest violence, someone had shot him clean in the head. That someone so much larger than life could be murdered shook Greg. If Kareem wasn't safe, who was?

To Greg, the fact that the trio of deaths that weekend reflected different ages, different lifestyles, sent a message: death was all-inclusive.

Greg was eager to get back home to be a part of what was unfolding in the city, but first he had to take care of his friend. The pain that John was feeling at the loss of his father was a microcosm of the pain being felt throughout the city, but to Greg, amid all the turmoil he was experiencing, it felt outsized. Besides, after the Saturday night dust-up back in Baltimore everybody was calling for peace, and he wasn't interested in taking part. He just didn't believe in standing arm in arm with the powerful politicians who for years had brokered their pain. A peaceful Baltimore was an oxymoron.

Nick

BALTIMORE CITY COUNCILMAN NICK MOSBY joined the rest of the congregation leaping to their feet as the Rev. Walter Thomas hit the climax of his sermon. New Psalmist was one of the largest congregations in Baltimore, a sanctuary where every Sunday close to seven thousand congregants came to listen to the word of God from Pastor Thomas's booming voice. As he spoke in his end-of-sermon cadence, his voice ascending, accompanied by rhythmic organ blasts, the congregation collectively, spontaneously rose. This sermon, "Right Person for the Right Time," especially resonated with Nick at this moment. Nick knew Baltimore. It was his birthplace, the place that raised him. This was a moment he'd been anticipating, the moment he'd come back home for.

Nick had grown up in a two-bedroom house with six women, raised by his mother, Eunice Orange, the matriarch of the family and the bulwark of Nick's life. Nick's father was a major presence in the city—everyone in Baltimore knew him. Everyone but Nick. Nick only met his father six times in his life. The last time had been when Nick was in ninth grade and his father showed up at Nick's new school in a brand-new black Cadillac. Pulling up slowly as Nick walked out of the school's main building at the end of the day, he stopped and rolled down the window. "Here you go, son," his father said as he handed Nick $1,000 in folded bills. Nick peered in through the car window. His father looked thin and frail; sunglasses hid his eyes. Nick took the money and wanted to say more, but once the money changed hands, the car quickly pulled off. Nick never saw his father again.

At that point Nick had just been accepted to Baltimore Polytechnic Institute, or "Poly," as it is known around the city. It is one of the oldest high schools in Baltimore, a selective school that students test into and need to work hard to stay in. Considering that Nick's first school had been Chinquapin Elementary—a school Baltimoreans called "Chicken Pen" before the city closed it down—going to a place like Poly was hardly foreordained for Nick. But he had a few things going for him. One was his incredibly inquisitive and analytical mind. Another was a persistent mother who only had a few rules for her son: be honest, take care of your family, and when you have the chance, *leave Baltimore.*

And so he did—at least for a while. After high school he went to historically black Tuskegee University in Alabama for an engineering degree. His mother believed that, armed with his degree and his enchanting smile, he was ready for bigger things than Baltimore could provide. She wanted him to see the world outside of Baltimore and never come back.

Baltimore had been home to the Mosbys for generations, and while the family's roots were there, pain lived there, too. Nick had the chance to chart a new destiny for their family.

After college he received job offers from all around the country, with the exception of one place: Baltimore City. But that's where he decided to go.

This time, though, he was not coming home alone. While in college he'd met a beautiful and ambitious young woman from Boston who aspired to be an attorney. Marilyn was from a tough neighborhood in Boston and wanted to start over in a city like Washington, DC, Atlanta, maybe Austin or Charlotte. A city that felt vibrant, like it was growing—a place where ambitions were limited only by your vision. Nick and Marilyn married in 2005, and she begged her husband to find work in one of the cities that was actively recruiting both of them. But Nick was persistent and certain. He wanted to come back to Baltimore. He wanted to be near his family. And he had a vision of his own: he wanted to one day be the mayor of the city he'd called home all his life. He'd seen growing up how elected officials had the power to either create change or stunt it. They led rallies or shut them down. Addressed pain or permitted it. Without a job offer, and watching his mother fight off tears, he and Marilyn made the decision to return to Charm City.

Now, at the end of the New Psalmist service, Nick looked down at his young daughters, the final two pieces of his Norman Rockwell–esque family portrait. When Nick had walked into church with his family that morning and greeted his fellow congregants, no one asked him about the day before, and the unrest. Nick had attended a half dozen marches over the past week. All of them had been peaceful, and, he felt, all of them had been productive. He was proud of Baltimore for taking pain and turning it into purpose, and was upset at the media for continuing to show a very small area of chaos and violence in a loop as if it represented the entire city. The violence was restricted to a few blocks and a handful of interactions, but you would think the conflict around the stadium defined the entire city. Where had the national media been when all of the peaceful marches were going on? Where was the media now, as the entire congregation celebrated together with joy and peace, no one talking about the events of the previous night? He didn't feel like the entire story was being told. His vision of Baltimore, the Baltimore that could be, the one he'd excitedly returned to years ago, was all around him in church. The Baltimore the media was portraying was a different one. It was the Baltimore his mother had warned him about, the one she never wanted him to return to.

Anthony

ANTHONY WILLIAMS SAT ON THE trapezoid-shaped concrete steps that guarded the glassy entrance of Baltimore City's premier roller-skating rink, his elbows weighing heavy on his knees, the brim of his baseball cap riding low. Twiddling his thumbs nervously, he leaned forward to look up and down the street, ears tuned to the unusual quiet of West Baltimore. The street was typically bathed in an ambient din at this time of the evening: kids playing, 92Q Jams blaring, sidewalk vendors and hustlers selling random merchandise on the street, cursing, laughter, sirens. Today, though, it was quiet.

The stairs he sat on were the perfect perch from which to watch the evolution of the surrounding neighborhood. Pennsylvania Avenue had been one of the true economic hubs of Baltimore in its glory days. Before the explosion of economic revitalization schemes like Inner Harbor, there was Pennsylvania Avenue, the main street of black Baltimore. Jazz clubs, doctors' offices, and the Sphinx Theatre; middle-class rowhouses physically and communally touching, with multicolored facades and captivating architectural flair that made each home distinct in a sea of connection. But eventually even the mecca of Pennsylvania Avenue fell. Its streetcars, shops, and vibrant movie theaters changed after the neighborhood was hollowed out by the 1968 riots sparked by the assassination of Dr. Martin Luther King Jr. Black-owned banks and clothing stores gave way to liquor stores and sneaker shops owned by Korean immigrants. Supermarkets were shuttered when their owners fled the inner city, replaced by small corner stores where all the goods were behind bulletproof plastic and customers had to yell through the barrier to ask for the packaged and processed food on the shelves.

There is a correlation between moments of unrest, like the ones in 1968, and what happens to the communities thereafter. As smoke fills the air, so does uncertainty. With uncertainty, investment flees. Indifference and control fill the space. It becomes tougher to get loans because banks either choose not to lend or make the lending requirements so prohibitive that ordinary shopkeepers and entrepreneurs find them impossible to navigate. Large capital infusions give way to smaller, back-door capital flows, making it challenging for local businesses to grow and sustain themselves. Insurance premiums jump. The cost of goods rises, making it more complicated for the community to participate economically and support their neighbors. If businesses don't grow, they don't hire. When they don't hire, more people have less. The conditions that led to the riots then become exacerbated because resources become more scarce.

By the time Anthony sat on those gray concrete steps in April 2015 listening for any signs of life, Pennsylvania had become one of the most violent streets in the city. But Anthony felt safe on those steps. They had saved his life.

Shake & Bake first opened its doors in 1982. Founded by

and named after former Baltimore Colts wide receiver and fan favorite Glenn "Shake & Bake" Doughty, it's both a roller-skating rink and a forty-lane bowling alley. In its over thirty years of operation, more than one million people have walked through its doors.

But no one seemed to be coming today.

"Mr. Ant!" Anthony heard the distinctive voice of Malik, the young man's pitched and elongated Baltimore accent ringing through the air. Malik was twenty-two, a West Baltimore kid with a skinny frame and a scraggly beard that covered much of the lower half of his face. Anthony knew that tattoos covered both of Malik's arms, but today they were hidden by a long-sleeved white T-shirt. The shirt didn't conceal the spray of tattoos on Malik's neck, though.

Anthony recruited kids in the community to come volunteer or work at Shake & Bake. He tried to find kids who might not have any other opportunities—the ones with hard histories or habits that made them unemployable at other places. These kids might have been spurned by other employers, but Anthony knew better. His recruits took the opportunity of mentorship and employment with Anthony seriously, because they knew that, for the moment at least, this might be the only chance they had. Anthony recognized these kids because thirty years ago he'd been one. That's what he saw in Malik: himself. That's why they understood each other.

Anthony raised his hand in acknowledgment as Malik sat down next to him, along with a few friends. He had been working inside, but apparently there wasn't much to do.

"It's crazy quiet in there tonight, crazy quiet," Malik said.

A soft "Yup" was all Anthony could muster in reply. Every Sunday night at Shake & Bake was adult skate night, and it was usually one of the most popular nights of the week. Close to three hundred people crowded in on a normal Sunday night. But only twenty-eight people, including Malik's friends scattered on the steps, had walked through the doors that evening. It was eerie. There was usually no time for sitting on steps on an adult skate night. Too much to do. Anthony and his small but loyal band of employees would have to staff the concession stand, the arcade area, the bowling alley downstairs, and the community room inside Shake & Bake that held everything from birthday parties to community meetings attended by City Council members. But tonight they had time to sit outside and talk.

"Hey, Mr. Ant, heard about what happened down at the Orioles' stadium?"

"Yeah, I heard. Bad, huh?"

Malik had been down there. As he began to describe what he saw, Anthony noticed that a smile appeared on his face.

"Worse than bad, man," Malik said. "They were lighting police cars on fire."

Another boy chimed in. "Yeah, I heard they were trying to storm the field and what not."

Anthony knew that rumors about what had happened yesterday were spreading like crazy, many of them exaggerations or flat-out fiction—but every rumor of chaos and anarchy and violence added to the thickening tension. It was palpable. And Anthony could see that the young people who really had witnessed last night's uprising were feeling emboldened. He could see it in Malik's smile tonight. Something had turned. The riot gear, the shields, the teargas—none of it seemed to have intimidated the crowd. They shouted out for accountability and weren't going to be turned away. They definitely weren't going to fall back in the name of "patience." Time was up, and no matter how well-armed and aggressive the police were, the kids kept coming.

In fact, the more militarized the police response, the more the community response escalated. The police, weighed down by their protective gear and military-grade weapons, seemed to conjure the violence all of that equipment was designed to confront. Anthony sat fascinated as the young boys explained the thrill of watching the police shrink from confrontation and give up their tactical positioning.

"They spend all day telling us to get off corners in our own communities," Malik said, still incredulous. "How you gonna do that? So watching them back up as we got closer, that felt crazy, man."

Jenny

Jenny Egan spent most of Sunday documenting what had happened the previous day. The night before, at least thirty protesters had been arrested—the first arrests to take place following the week of unrest after the news broke that Freddie was gone.

Jenny, whose day job was as a public defender in the juvenile justice system, was working jail support, part of the grassroots legal system that had begun taking shape across the city, staffed by volunteer lawyers like Jenny. Lawyers from across the country had started pouring into the city earlier that week, once advertisements about the big march began to spread. She was among the nearly one hundred people who had gathered by ten o'clock Saturday morning at the University of Baltimore Law School for training on how to support the protesters by observing, planning, watching, and waiting to leap into action.

Baltimore lawyers welcomed the help of the Ferguson Legal Defense Committee, whose high-profile lawyers, like human rights attorney Nicole Lee, had been on the front line of protests in Ferguson after the death of Mike Brown. The attorneys brought experience in mass arrest and police tactics, and partnered with local attorneys who brought their knowledge of Baltimore's system, fanning out across the city to different points along the march route.

Jenny stayed behind at a local law firm's offices at Charles and Pratt Streets, setting up a jail support system—creating a hotline number, a database, secure networks, and protocols, teaching volunteers how the arrest and bail system works in Baltimore. Jenny didn't know how to prepare for a full-fledged uprising, but she knew what injustice looked like in Baltimore.

Protesting police violence was what she did for a living. She stood before judges every day, defending clients who often looked a lot like Freddie Gray against charges brought by officers who engaged in the same patterns of abuse that were now being exposed. For years she watched these tactics, like the one they called "plug and play" that helped them evade accountability through simply plugging in the same narrative to justify arrests. The police report narratives always contained some semblance of the same—*"In my training and experience, XX movement is related to XXX criminal activity"*—no matter how benign the act might be. Jenny always thought that the police might as well save themselves the trouble and just write, *"In my training and experience, black kids are criminals."* As a public defender, she had seen the worst of the city in the way it treats its children. If a kid made it to Jenny, it meant that every other system had failed—housing, education, health. Her office is located in the Baltimore City Juvenile Justice Center, famously called "Baby Booking."

When the news had broken a week earlier that Freddie Gray had died, Jenny took it hard. Anger consumed her. She thought about the kids who had been shot by police in

Maryland—a fourteen-year-old shot while playing in an empty apartment, a nineteen-year-old who was being attacked by a dog when they shot him. She thought about how things could have been different if there had been a video of the arrest of Tyrone West, whose sister she'd watched for years on television and on social media as Tawanda cried "No justice, no peace" into what seemed like an abyss.

And now Freddie was dead. She just couldn't believe the police had killed another person. As much as she resented the media's relentless coverage of his death and the protests that ensued, she was glad that the constant exposure kept his death in front of viewers nationwide and beyond. She was used to stories of police killings not making the paper at all, let alone looping on repeat on international news for the world to see. She watched the video of Freddie's arrest over and over again. While others across the country were doing that, too, analyzing the contortions of Freddie's body while he was being dragged to the police van and listening to his screams, Jenny was watching for a different reason. She was staring at the police officers' faces.

They're going to get away with it, she thought.

Jenny had attended days of protests since April 19, the day that Freddie died. She had even written an email to all of her elected officials, urging them to join her:

As my representatives, I wanted to reach out to you to say that I've been disappointed that I have not seen legislative and city council leadership at the Freddie Gray protests.

Police corruption and police brutality are systemic problems in Baltimore. I am writing to ask for more than police body cameras, but real legislative reform to end "jump outs" or stop-and-frisk in Maryland and legislative reform to the LEO [Law Enforcement Officers'] Bill of Rights and use of force guidelines.

Additionally, community members, activists, families, students, and victims of police brutality are meeting today at 3 PM at City Hall. Your presence at these protests and your leadership on these matters are requested.

Please join us and speak out against police brutality in no uncertain terms.

But Saturday was different. On that night, the protesters had decided that no longer would they wait for anyone to speak for them. Jenny watched from the sidewalk as the police, with their riot gear, came face-to-face with a swarming fearlessness they had not seen before. The protesters had damn near taken over downtown, washing over a part of the city that often tries to block them out. Not even a baseball game at Camden Yards, a rare point of solidarity in a fractured city, was enough to keep things civil. Even with all the arrests, the protesters had sent a clear warning that this wasn't the end of it: they chanted over and over again, "No justice, no peace."

Jenny had spent the night watching, waiting for the increasingly irritated police officers to strike. At the first sign of an arrest, she ran back to the legal hub, ready to spring into action. She feared that same narrative of police abuse and impunity would play out again, especially as the police vans pulled up. One of those had taken Freddie for his last ride, finding every curve and bump until Freddie was in a coma—what they called a "rough ride." The sight of the vans triggered a panic in Jenny. Would the same fate befall any of the protesters now being rounded up?

The legal observers had printed hotline numbers on flyers,

handing them out en masse, and had written the numbers in black Sharpie down their forearms. As protesters were cuffed and lifted into the back of the vans, the legal observers would hold out their arms for the arrestees to see, while shouting the phone number to call. On the other end of the line during their first phone call would be Jenny, who was waiting for them.

Partee

PARTEE WOKE UP SUNDAY MORNING on a brown futon in his office. His night had ended just five hours before, at two-thirty in the morning. That futon was not made for a man of his size; his legs hung over the edge and one of his arms drooped over the side. But it wouldn't have mattered much where he lay down, as he wouldn't have slept much that night anyway.

His wife, Cecelia, had texted him when she saw the intensity of the conflict in downtown Baltimore, and he'd dashed off a quick reply: *I'm OK*. She didn't press for more. They usually communicated with each other multiple times a day, but on hard days, days like yesterday, she knew better than to expect much of a response from him. She wouldn't complain; she knew it was what she had signed up for when she married a police officer, because her own father had been one. Plus, she didn't have to get the news from him, as her television was on all night. She knew what kind of evening it was.

He wanted to talk to her, unload some of what he was going through, but he couldn't. He was consumed with thoughts about what had been one of the most chaotic nights of his entire tenure as a member of the Baltimore Police Department. The chaos outside had stirred up chaos inside, too—the emotions that swirled in him were complicated and contradictory. He was upset with the young people he'd watched hurling debris and destroying police cars the night before. But he was also upset that it had come to this. And he was upset that he understood exactly why they'd been throwing bricks.

Partee had joined the police force two decades ago because he wanted to do his part to heal the disconnect between police and the West Baltimore community he grew up in. He'd seen the fissures between police and residents firsthand growing up, but he still felt deeply that there was no way any of his colleagues would have intentionally killed Freddie Gray. He couldn't conceive of any of them waking up that morning with homicide on their minds. But he also understood why this was tougher for the rest of the community to believe. Their anger was real, and so was their skepticism. Partee felt it was unfair for him and his brothers and sisters in arms to be blamed for the horrid conditions that they were now being asked to come in and police. How do you police a failed school system? How do you police an unemployment rate that hovers around 50 percent for African American men between the ages of eighteen and thirty-five? How do you police an opioid epidemic that needs to have a public health solution and not a criminal justice one? He also knew that the police department he and his colleagues worked for, by retaining and defending discriminatory policing practices that even the United States Department of Justice found routinely violated the constitutional rights of residents, such as conducting unlawful stops and using excessive force, was part of the reason for the torrid conditions.

Partee hadn't initially wanted to be a cop at first. After finishing college at Morgan State, he decided he wanted to be a teacher. He interned for a while at Robert Poole Middle School, a public school nestled in a working-class neighborhood. The school was—rather appropriately, he thought—situated between an elevated expressway and Johns Hopkins University, two paths out of the neighborhood. People say you know pretty early whether or not teaching is right for you, and sure enough, Partee learned pretty quickly it was not his calling.

He also worked at the Fudgery, a legendary candy shop located at the heart of the Inner Harbor, where fudge-making is accompanied by singing and dancing. Tell them it's your birthday, and your decadent fudge offering will be coupled with a pitch-perfect a capella rendering of "Happy Birthday" (both the classic version and the "black" version—Stevie Wonder's tribute to Martin Luther King Jr. Day). The members of the Baltimore-bred R&B singing group Dru Hill, named after a famous park in West Baltimore, met while working together at the Fudgery. Everyone who works at the Fudgery has the same job: candy maker. And the application process is anything but traditional. Applicants have to demonstrate an understanding of math, science (to make the candy), and musical pitch. Therefore, to get the job not only did Partee have to show he could make a mean batch of fudge, but he also had to show off his tenor vocal range.

The Fudgery was also where he'd met Cecelia. She always said that Partee reminded her of her father, a burly and kind man who believed deeply in family and in community. Cecelia's cousin Cassandra had been a career Baltimore police officer, and Cecelia's stories about her cousin became an early model for Partee. Partee's family had its own legacy of service—he grew up admiring how his grandfather, a Marine, always took pride in his dress and sense of discipline. How he held his shoulders back and his chest out. Partee had considered joining the Marines right out of high school and was on his way to the recruiting station when he received an acceptance letter from Morehouse College. But it was conversations with his grandfather Grandpa Joe that had gotten Partee interested in the police department in the first place.

"Anybody can talk. Not many do. What are you going to do to change things?" Partee remembers the exact words his grandfather said to the aimless young Fudgery employee. And it could not have come at a more perfect time. That young man was seeking direction. Grandpa Joe's push, and Cassandra's example of life as a career police officer, provided both.

As Partee started to get up from the futon on this late April morning, he was surrounded by artifacts of a useful life: pictures of his family, certificates and awards he had received in his twenty years of service on the force. He looked up and saw a framed poem that he had first encountered while a student at Morehouse, written by its former president, Benjamin E. Mays. Mays had preached nonviolent civil resistance and mentored leaders such as Dr. King and Maynard Jackson. After last night, Partee realized, the poem had taken on a new meaning.

Didn't seek it, didn't choose it
But it's up to me to use it
I must suffer if I lose it

John

O<small>N</small> S<small>UNDAY MORNING</small> J<small>OHN AROSE</small> early. No alarm clock needed. He hadn't really slept the night before. Here he was in the middle of a vacation he had been looking forward to all year, and the only thing he could think about was ending it. He woke Margaret and told her he needed to head home. She didn't like it, but she understood.

Three hundred sixty-five miles. The distance from his vacation home in upstate New York to Baltimore. Saratoga Springs was his wife's hometown, and over the years, he'd gotten as comfortable there as she was. It was quiet and green—he loved the peace and calm. The distance from home and its worries. But he needed to return home, back to a city on fire.

He wasn't sure what he would find there once he arrived or what he was supposed to do, but he knew how he had to present himself for the sake of the team—and maybe for the sake of the city. He wanted to seem indomitable, a rock that would help focus those around him on returning to a sense of normalcy. The protests had been going on for a couple of weeks, and he felt so deeply for the Gray family. But it was also a game day. He told himself to remember the purity of baseball. Why people love the game so much. The escape. The lifelong family memories. A place apart from whatever conflicts are tearing us apart outside the park. Something simple in a complicated world. But how to keep things feeling established when the eyes of the people he walked past on the way to the ballpark reflected such brokenness?

Jenny

JENNY HAD A LOT IN common with the young black teens she called clients. She and they had grown up worlds apart—Tangent, Oregon, for her, Baltimore, Maryland, for them—but they spoke the same language: pain, chaos, tarnished optimism. She was the daughter of teenagers, who themselves were the children of teenagers, and she'd narrowly escaped continuing the cycle. She came from a line of Okies, farm families from the Southern Plains who'd migrated to California in the 1930s to escape economic and environmental catastrophes caused by the Great Depression and the Dust Bowl, and even when her family settled down in Oregon they were never really settled. Her grandmother, the matriarch, had a seventh-grade education and grew up in and out of foster care and orphanages before giving birth to Jenny's mother, Vickie, at sixteen. Jenny admired her mother and father. Vickie and Jim had begun having kids in high school and raised a total of seven children—five of their own and two cousins. Jenny's parents were determined to give them a better life, but in the early years focused much of that energy on bettering themselves. Her father was intent on going to college, even signing up for the military so that he could get GI Bill benefits to pay for his classes. To his family's initial chagrin, he left a good job at the beef jerky plant—and its steady paycheck and benefits—to go back to school. But soon after, others in the family followed his example—even Jenny's grandmother, Mae, who prided herself on working at the US Postal Service but, inspired by her son, got her GED at age sixty.

Though education became the focal point of her family's life, Jenny grew up angry. While her parents had created a road map to success, they took detours. Her mother and father, as much as they loved their children, were kids raising kids, and their children witnessed and absorbed their immature and volatile relationship.

Jenny's anger and anxiety showed up at school—she was a self-described "weirdo" and had a lot of disciplinary problems. She got kicked out a lot, mostly for busting heads. It was an outlet for her rage and already woven into the culture she grew up in. In rural America, like the inner city, fighting is how you dealt with problems, and she was a good problem-solver.

Nothing scared her until her junior year, when she turned sixteen and the pregnancy test read positive. She saw her whole life, the best and worst parts of what her family had shown her, flash before her eyes.

She drove forty-five minutes to Salem, Oregon, where there was a Planned Parenthood, only to discover when she got there that the doctor traveled to that location from Portland once a month and that wasn't the day. The nurses told her to come back in three days or else she'd have to wait one more month, and by then it would be too late.

Her parents had staked so many of their hopes on their children and given them all the advantages they hadn't had: a two-parent household, a stable place to live. And if Jenny went through with the pregnancy, she would be carrying on the one family tradition they had tried to leave behind. She could see it, that life as a teenage mother, and in some respects it would have been easy. She had models. She could be good at doing nothing, surrounded by children, steeping in self-hate. But part of her wanted more.

She'd watched the effects of teenage pregnancy do some crazy things to the people she loved. The person she'd known the longest in her life had had her first child at fourteen, and another before she graduated from high school; she went to night school and got her GED, but struggled with drugs and addiction and was in and out of prison.

Jenny started a new life the day she ended that pregnancy. Within weeks, the seventeen-year-old was flipping through a 1991 edition of a college guidebook looking for an escape route. She measured out three thousand miles on a map as her compass, and circled all the colleges in the book that were three thousand miles away from Tangent. She wrote them letters on a typewriter, asking for brochures and fee waivers. She applied to every school that would allow her to do so for free, including Howard, though she had never heard of an HBCU, a historically black college or university.

She got even more gutsy and decided she wanted to go visit these colleges. She traveled around town asking dentists and car dealerships to sponsor her on a college trip, collecting $50 here and $100 there. All told, she raised $1,850, and booked her own plane tickets and hotels.

It was on those college visits that she had her first brush with true elitism, and it was a rude awakening. Her first stop was Barnard College, where she learned that her Dockers and white button-down shirt didn't qualify as business casual. The admissions officers' eyes told her so, and it wasn't long before hers welled up with tears as she fled the office. It was the first time she felt less than, and it would be the last.

She landed at Smith College because they were nice to her. Her application conveyed a troubled student, by some accounts another statistic. But they gave her a chance. Most likely because she had something that the black teens she now represented did not: white skin.

Billy

O F THE FOUR V AUGHN G REENE funeral homes in the Baltimore region, the one in North Baltimore was the busiest. The manicured lawn and cared-for architectural structure sat not far from where Freddie Gray spent his last moments of freedom. That Sunday, as the sun shone on the funeral home, the sun at about its highest point blessing the whole city with late spring sunshine, Billy Murphy slowly walked up the stone stairs and through the white-painted wooden doors with clean glass panes that allowed the natural light to illuminate the inside.

Billy had been to countless wakes before. Wakes of clients whose legacy he was left to defend, fighting for those left behind. Wakes of so many who'd met their demise at the hands of their neighbors, friends, and family, shot down by dope boys, gangsters, and, yes, police. Billy was tired of wakes, but it was part of his job description at this point.

Billy peered around the room and saw a kaleidoscope of Baltimore. Preachers wearing their Sunday best stood alongside young men in their early twenties with their pants barely holding on. Billy locked eyes with Freddie Gray's stepfather, Richard "Rick" Shipley, who had become the unofficial spokesperson for the family. He was not even sixty, but his slight frame and worn face reminded Billy of a man well past that age. But Rick was rock solid—he understood what was at stake at this fragile moment and his role in it. He'd grown up knowing all about police brutality and was as sick of it as anyone, especially now that it had touched his life so intimately. But he also understood that the emotions of the moment could undermine any movement toward justice, and he tried to represent the family with as much grace and dignity as he could muster given the pain they were all in. As Billy and Rick embraced, Billy held him tightly, knowing the weight that now sat on Rick's shoulders. Sitting in the corner of the crowded room was Freddie's mother, slumped over in her chair with her eyes closed. Billy hoped she was praying but wondered if she was high, sitting just a few feet away from her son's cold body. Freddie's mother wrestled with addiction much of her life, a war that Billy knew she still waged. And he knew the pressure of the past weeks had not been easy—it was the kind of pain that might have made the battle for sobriety seem more daunting than the horrors of addiction. Billy turned to look around the room, his heart heavy. The scene he'd walked into epitomized so much of the crisis that he now found himself in the middle of.

As Billy moved through the adopted sanctuary, his gray ponytail swinging from side to side, people stepped aside in deference, nodded in acknowledgment, or hugged him in appreciation. Not only was Billy the newly selected counsel representing the Gray family, he was one of the best-known lawyers in Baltimore. The combination of his bright smile and razor-sharp understanding of the law drew people in crisis to

him. He was a great person to have on your side. They also respected the legacy he represented. He was the great-grandson
of John H. Murphy Sr., the founder and publisher of the *Afro-
American*. Based in Baltimore, the *Afro* is the longest-running
family-owned African American newspaper in the nation, the
flagship of a chain of papers in more than a dozen cities. Since
1892, black families have paged through the paper for news,
opinions, and a celebration of blackness.

The Murphy name meant something in Baltimore. And
getting Billy Murphy to represent you meant something in
that city. It meant you had not only the best chance at winning
a case, but also the best chance of being heard. And it was the
reason the Gray family reached out to him so early.

Billy moved toward the front of the hall until he saw Freddie in his casket. He walked over and touched Freddie's stiff
arm. Billy was not a religious man, but he took a moment to
say a quick prayer for Freddie. The first time Billy had seen his
client, Freddie was in a coma. Now Billy stared at his body,
frozen and soulless. He never had a single conversation with
Freddie Gray, but somehow he could hear Freddie speaking to
him. *I'm ready for this*, Freddie said to him. *Buckle up*.

Anthony

HIS FIRST JOB AT SHAKE & Bake was as a "punch kid," the worker who would take tickets as people entered the Bake. He was promoted right around the same time he got sober. Shake & Bake's management saw something in Anthony, a natural leadership ability and an understanding of how the business worked. The biggest obstacle to Anthony's success was Anthony. Could he show up on time? Could he quit his addiction and stop letting it run his decision-making? Many people tried to help him, but it was his grandparents, whom he called Dollbaby and Grandpop, who finally held an intervention for Anthony. "They told me they knew I would be gone if I didn't get right. They worried they would lose me and I would throw away my future." He knew it was them, them and Shake & Bake, that saved him.

He often thought back to the day he'd first shown up there looking for a job. He was nineteen and desperate for work. A part-time job, temp work, anything that could provide some income, which he needed to support the heroin and cocaine addiction he'd first developed in eighth grade at Herring Run

Junior High School in Northeast Baltimore. The same addiction that clouded his entire high school experience until he was informed by his math teacher that he was going to fail and would not be permitted to graduate. Anthony couldn't figure out how he could possibly fail math. He *loved* math, loved numbers. He had a natural knack for analyzing and retaining statistics. So the surprise to him was not just that he wasn't passing a class he'd always loved, but how far gone in his drug addiction he was that he hadn't seen it coming.

But once he got the gig at Shake & Bake he kicked his drug habit, his life anchored by his work at the skating rink. He had held almost every position at Shake & Bake and was now general manager, the one in charge of everything. He *was* Shake & Bake, for all intents and purposes, and had been so for years. For close to nineteen years he had been in charge of all operations at Shake & Bake, and this East Baltimore boy had very much become one of Pennsylvania Avenue's most recognizable faces. He thought by now he'd seen it all from those white steps. But he was wrong.

John

As John walked around outside the stadium he'd personally watched being built, brick by brick, he felt like a foreigner. He'd passed places where less than twenty-four hours earlier people had been standing on top of police cars, smashing windows, and chanting "All night, all day, we will fight for Freddie Gray."

He knew that around 6:00 P.M. the day before, protesters had crossed paths with a small group of baseball fans outside Pickles Pub, a stalwart sports bar right outside the ballpark. It wasn't clear who started it—there were different accounts floating around. But the story John heard from his team was that protesters began yelling "Black lives matter" while a few of the fans angrily yelled back "We don't care." Then some of those at the bar started yelling out racial epithets at the protesters. Interactions like these had been reported at other spots near the ballpark—Frank and Nic's, Sliders—where the combination of drunk fans and angry protesters created a commotion.

John thought about his grandfather, after whom he'd been

named, as he walked the grounds. His grandfather and great-uncle had owned a produce company in Baltimore City beginning in the 1960s. Every morning, starting at four o'clock, the two of them would drive all around the city and county delivering tomatoes, lettuce, onions, and cabbage to area bars, taverns, and restaurants. They'd travel the full breadth of the city, from some of its poorest areas to its wealthiest. And the elder John Angelos had talked to everyone, whether they were loading staff or store owners, black waitstaff or white refrigeration crews. John's first job, when he was fourteen years old, had been to ride around and help with the drop-offs. The thing that John remembered and admired most was the fact that his grandfather could have great conversations with anybody. He knew about their families, their struggles, their hopes. No matter what was going on, his grandfather could coax a smile out of anyone.

As John walked around the exterior of Camden Yards, stepping on shattered glass, he thought about what his grandfather would say.

Partee

Zion Baptist Church sat on the 1700 block of Caro-line Street, in the center of East Baltimore. The gray stone Gothic-style building, constructed in 1956, sits almost squarely between the National Great Blacks in Wax Museum and Green Mount Cemetery. Zion had been Partee's wife's childhood church and was now their family church. It was quite a distance from where Partee lived, but it was the place that spoke to him. He felt a sense of belonging there. A community.

That Sunday he was excited to go to church. Instead of going all the way home first, he just told his wife to meet him there. She told him they should skip the service that Sunday— that after the night he'd had, he should just come home, shower, and rest. Maybe finally talk about what happened. But Partee needed to go to church, to a place where he felt welcomed and loved. A place where people were not yelling at him, cursing at him, blaming him. He put on his black suit, the suit he kept in his office for "just in case" moments like this. He thought that the suit and black tie made him look like he was on his way to a funeral, which that morning seemed fitting.

For the past week he'd felt waves of anger from the community washing over the Baltimore police—him included. Partee wished he could have told them that he was from their community. He wished he could have pushed Pause and sat them down and explained everything. But he still felt unsure about what exactly he would have explained.

The church seemed unusually quiet when he walked in that Sunday; apparently many in the congregation had stayed home. And Partee felt like everyone who was there was staring at him. He felt like things got real quiet when he walked in, as if everyone had been talking about him and the conversation abruptly ended once he entered. Partee had never felt so uncomfortable in a place that had always given him so much consolation.

He sat down, opened his Police Officer's Bible, and began reading, the leather-bound book of scripture with a faded police shield on its cover serving as his armor. Now and again he glanced up and tried to meet the skeptical stares with a smile, but he felt like his skin was burning. He turned to his favorite scripture, Matthew 5:16: "In the same way, let your light shine before others so that they may see your good works and give glory to your Father who is in Heaven." He read it over and over again because it moved him—but also because he didn't want to lift his head up.

Billy

Billy Murphy is Baltimore. Born and raised in the city, he is the son of an activist mother and a judge father and followed in their footsteps, spending a lifetime in civil rights advocacy and using the law to advocate for black people and the disenfranchised. His signature ponytail and profanity-laced tirades have been staples in Baltimore politics for decades. In 1980, he was elected to Baltimore's circuit court, Maryland's highest trial court, but after a few years as a judge he made the decision that true social momentum in the city came only through two angles, politics and business. So in 1983 he decided to take on the popular incumbent mayor, William Donald Schaefer, in what became one of the most memorable races in recent Baltimore history.

Schaefer served in public life for over fifty years, holding municipal and statewide seats including City Council member, City Council president, mayor, governor, and comptroller. He was a lifelong Baltimorean—Baltimore was the only home he knew, with the exception of his time as a military officer, which brought him around the world in uniform. He came back to Baltimore after his service in the military, received his law degree, and in 1971 became the mayor of the city of his birth.

Known for his "do it now" approach as mayor, he became synonymous with the improvements in downtown Baltimore, helping to reshape the image of Baltimore and turning it into a true tourism magnet for out-of-towners. But for Billy, Schaefer was responsible for the rapid inequality that had also become a Baltimore staple. Billy saw how blacks in his community would be locked up for the same offenses that people in other communities would be protected from. He remembered how he'd gone to a Grateful Dead concert and been blown away to see that everyone in the crowd was openly smoking marijuana, when he knew a young black man doing the same exact thing would be met with handcuffs instead of acceptance. Where the actions of some were tolerated, the actions of others were patrolled. Billy felt Schaefer was responsible for the parts of Baltimore that the wealthy shunned and where the poor were told that they were the problem. While Schaefer ran on a platform of "worth repeating," Murphy ran on a platform of "the other Baltimore."

Billy paid Patrick Caddell, a pollster who'd worked for Jimmy Carter, $19,000 to come work for him. This was a lot of money in 1983 for a pollster, particularly for a mayor's race. The tall, brawny Caddell was known for being one of the best in the business. He was also known as a renegade who oftentimes found himself at odds with the Democratic establishment, so much so that his career eventually shifted toward working with conservative outlets, garnering him the nickname "Fox News Democrat." Famously, he also warned that Democrats shouldn't avoid speaking to issues of economic insecurity, and in the late 1970s he predicted that an outsider candidate could tap into that fear, upend both political parties, and win the presidency.

Schaefer had a 90 percent approval rating in the city, but Caddell assured Billy that he too had a favorable image and that he had a clear path to victory. In a city that was 75 percent African American, all Billy needed to do was to get African Americans to support him and the numbers would inevitably put him over the top. But on election day, Billy lost the race by forty-six points. It was a landslide, with Schaefer earning more than 70 percent of the vote.

Billy was flabbergasted. African Americans represented such a high percentage of the city's residents, and he had been explicit about how his mayoralty was going to impact African Americans, while Schaefer could not articulate why blacks should vote for him, so how did Schaefer win so handily? When he asked Caddell that question, Caddell told him, "You have to understand, you didn't have a credible white man to vouch for you." He explained that Billy needed a white man to vouch for him not because that person would help white people feel comfortable with Billy, but because it would help black people feel comfortable with Billy. He concluded with a simple phrase: "The white man's ice is colder." When he saw Billy's quizzical expression, Caddell shared the story that back in the day when iceboxes were used for refrigeration, one of the most popular ice companies, owned by a white man, hired a black man to work delivering ice. The boss would not let him deliver ice in the white community, only in the black community. This delivery person developed a wonderful rapport with the community that he did serve, and it helped him decide that once he was able to save up enough money and build his own ice delivery business, he would sell his ice cheaper and take all of the other company's business for himself. Years later he found a way to buy ice wholesale and began selling that ice to the black community at a lower price. But after months of work he realized he had only 25 percent of the business, and he could not understand why. He went to one of his friends who owned an auto business down the street and said, "I don't get it. My community loves me, and I am selling my ice to them at a fraction of the cost of the other companies, but I am still only getting 25 percent of the business, while the white man's business is still getting 75 percent. What's going on?" His friend looked at him and said, "I hate to tell you this, son, but the word is out that the white man's ice is colder."

Billy understood what Caddell was trying to tell him, but he still mourned his electoral loss, hurt both by the margin of the loss and that the skepticism it symbolized came not from the white community but from his own.

Anthony

O N PENNSYLVANIA AVENUE, THE SLOGAN was "Shake &
Bake saves lives."

Despite working in the center of West Baltimore, Anthony
had been born in what seems like the other part of the world
for many West Baltimore residents, East Baltimore. Baltimore
is as territorial a city as you'll ever come across. It's a place
where "Where'd you go to school?" means the high school you
went to, and where the side of town you're from can tell the
questioner everything they need to know about you even before the real conversation commences. But Anthony's family
had moved a lot when he was a kid, going from Duncan Street
to Patterson Park to Federal Street, all before Anthony was in
middle school. That's why he was always able to adjust to
West Baltimore so well. He never felt like an outsider.

At its peak, Baltimore City had dozens of places where
young people could go to laugh, smile, enjoy themselves, and
escape for a while from the increasing chaos around them. But
there were only three roller-skating rinks. Fun City sat in a
firmly working-class residential area of Baltimore City, where

it was virtually the only family recreation activity nearby. Hot Skates was in Woodlawn, still in Baltimore County but just west of the city limits. For a long time Baltimore City had been a thriving economic engine and Baltimore County was the sleepy commuter retreat, but over the years the county had grown significantly in population and economic impact and activity, while the city saw its population decline greatly, losing more residents than any other major American jurisdiction except Detroit and Cleveland.

Located about seven miles southeast of Hot Skates, Shake & Bake was the busiest of all the rinks and the one that was most connected with the skating scene in Baltimore. Inside Shake & Bake you'd find some of the features of a traditional skating rink: colored lights, thumping dance music (hip-hop, R&B, and what was known as "Baltimore club music," a brilliant if overplayed mix of house music, Auto-Tune, and drum and bass), and, for the past thirty years, Anthony Williams.

Despite the deteriorating condition of the community outside its walls, business at Shake & Bake had stayed relatively stable for a long time. But revenue dipped significantly after the death of Freddie Gray and the subsequent marches. Anthony felt a looming concern about how long this dip would last. He was starting to think about the balance sheet in two distinct parts: BFG and AFG, before Freddie Gray and after Freddie Gray.

Anthony did not own Shake & Bake; in fact, the owner of Shake & Bake was the City of Baltimore, although it had been founded by Glenn "Shake & Bake" Doughty. The center relied not only on foot traffic but also on municipal business, as Doughty was able to secure a contract with the Baltimore City Public School System that drove students and dollars to the center. In partnership with Mayor Schaefer, Anthony created a space where the city supported something that all parties felt added value to the community.

Then in 1983 Doughty allowed the person challenging Schaefer for the mayor's office, Billy Murphy, to use the center for a fundraiser. Doughty didn't endorse Billy Murphy and he did not even attend the fundraiser, but since Murphy wanted to hold an event in the community and requested use of the space because it was central to the area and large enough to hold all the people Billy wanted to attend, Doughty obliged. Schaefer got wind of the decision and saw it as a tacit endorsement of Billy, and though Doughty pleaded with the mayor that this was not the case, Schaefer never forgot. When Shake & Bake's contract with the city came up for renewal, Doughty was met with a rejection.

That contract with the city had been his most significant source of revenue, and without it, Doughty knew there was no way he could sustain the business as a privately owned entity. In 1984 Doughty lost control of the business, and the new owner, the City of Baltimore Parks and Recreation Department, took over. While Doughty's nickname remained, Anthony was well aware of who the real boss was now.

That Sunday in April 2015, Anthony reluctantly shared with Malik and some other young men a conversation he'd had earlier in the day with Sgt. Fleet, a Baltimore City police officer whose beat included Shake & Bake. Fleet had stopped by Shake & Bake to give Anthony some advice: prepare for more violence. He told Anthony that some neighboring stores had taken his warnings very seriously, boarding up their windows and closing, as if the cop were a meteorologist predicting a storm heading up the Chesapeake. Anthony didn't want to believe that any violence could ever touch Shake & Bake, but he asked the boys for their thoughts.

Malik thought about it for a moment. "Gonna get worse. Things getting bad, man. Been hearing things gonna pop off tomorrow."

Anthony listened to his guys, but he felt like maybe everyone was overreacting. He had seen this before. Black Baltimore had had moments in the past when frustration peaked, but it had always burned itself out and vanished back underground, back into people's bodies and minds and homes, where it would manifest itself in ways that didn't make headlines or scare wealthier communities. This was probably another one of those moments, Anthony thought—the pain and anger weren't going to disappear, but they were going to go back underground. And Anthony couldn't afford to close anyway—revenue was revenue, even if less of it was coming in. He couldn't shut down just because there might be protests. His business couldn't survive that level of caution. Maybe most important to Anthony was that the family of Freddie Gray had asked for something different. They asked for calm, and peace, and reflection, all simultaneous with their quest for justice. Justice and peace.

For the moment the neighborhood's streets were quiet, as were Anthony, Malik, and the other young men. Anthony knew that maybe his hopes were naive; in the recesses of his mind he could still hear Freddie's screams as he was loaded into the back of the police van, along with the screams of the many mothers who over the years had received word that their children had been the victim of gun violence in that very neighborhood.

Then Malik broke the silence.

"All I know is ain't no way they gon' burn the Bake. We got you, Mr. Ant."

Greg

GREG DRAGGED HIMSELF HOME IN a drunken daze after a somber night out on the block with the boys talking about life and death. There didn't seem much he could say to console John after his father's death; to make matters worse, John had just had a daughter who now was going to grow up without a grandfather. Greg had never been good at consolation and didn't believe in the clichés that rang hollow in the hood—"Time heals all" and "This too shall pass"—so he helped John chase down his grief with fifths of Hennessy.

It was about one in the morning when he got home. Greg crept to his room in the dark, snapped on the lamp, and sat on his bed in silence. His mind was racing, and he took to googling on his phone, as he often did, to wind down for bed. He swiped through webpages about the drug war, about police and endangered communities. It was sort of an obsession of his to research such topics, looking for the context in which he existed. He believed he had a deep connection to the city, that its life was intertwined with his. And, as a history buff, he believed that nothing happened in a vacuum. He believed that no one moment changes the course of history; rather, hundreds of small moments lead up to a flash point. He often thought about the Soviet Union and how its dissolution had nothing to do with its foreign policy; rather, it had crumbled from inside. Baltimore was on the same path.

With murder on his mind, he began looking at homicide rates in Baltimore City. Eventually he came to a chart of those rates. It showed that the peak year for murders had been 1993—the year he was born.

Gregory Lee Butler Jr. was born on October 19 at Union Memorial Hospital to a complicated couple, Gerlena Jackson and Gregory Lee Butler Sr., who were by most accounts doing well despite living in a fracturing city. His parents never married but lived as a nuclear family in Charles Village. Charles Village was a perennially transitional community that was the birthplace of both Johns Hopkins University and discriminatory housing tract tactics in the United States. The average income in that area was one of the higher in the city because of its location near the university, but over a third of the community's residents were unemployed.

Greg's parents held down decent jobs. Both parents worked for Aegon, a large insurance company that in 1999 acquired the well-known insurance provider Transamerica. His mother worked in the kitchen of the company's cafeteria and his father had worked his way up from maintenance man to HVAC mechanic. They were employed and happy. In Baltimore, that's about as close to normal as you can get.

By the time Greg was born, the crack epidemic was in full force. For at least several years, his parents seemed to escape it. But when he was four, money started disappearing, and his parents began to fight about finances. They ended up moving from their oasis in Charles Village to Preston Street in the

Oliver neighborhood. His mother's behavior became more erratic, and when Greg was six, his father decided that he couldn't be around any activity that would put him, an exconvict, at risk of going back to prison, away from his children. So he moved out of the home to build a new life for them. Greg was told that they had different priorities and were no longer comfortable as a couple. They separated, and Greg figured out that it was because his mother had developed another relationship—with drugs.

The years on Preston Street were rough. Greg saw his father at least once a month but still had to learn to fend for himself. He had no choice: his mother started to go missing for days at a time. By around five years old, Greg started cooking on the stove, doing laundry, locking the door behind himself, finishing his homework, washing dishes, ironing clothes, and getting himself ready for school the next day. To this day, he can't stand the taste of Oodles of Noodles, and blames his childhood menu of hot dogs and hot sauce for his high blood pressure.

As his family fractured, Greg found a second family in his neighbors, the Dawsons. Greg loved his older sisters, Cameal and Serena, but he yearned for brothers. Almost immediately, he and the Dawsons' young boys, close to his age, became inseparable. They took on Baltimore together, playing on the basketball court and playground at Dr. Bernard Harris Sr. Elementary School. They rode their bikes throughout the city, from the Latrobe projects all the way down to the waterfront. They even got into trouble together, for stealing blunts and cigarettes from their older brothers. Greg drew the first smoke into his lungs at the age of six.

In 2002, just three days before his ninth birthday, Greg's second family fell victim to one of the most horrific crimes that Baltimore had ever seen. Angela and Carnell Dawson were the parents of five young children—parents who had repeatedly called the police about the drug dealers on their corner of East Baltimore, where persistent violence had shadowed the neighborhood for decades. On October 3, 2002, their home was firebombed, but they survived, although police were not able to find the person responsible. On October 15, the Dawsons made their last call to the police about neighborhood drug dealing. Vengeance arrived less than forty-eight hours later. Darrell Brooks had been a former page for the Baltimore City Council, a prestigious assignment, but had at some point been pulled into the drug game. He was on probation when he firebombed the Dawsons' house a second time, burning the mother and kids alive and fatally injuring their father.

Billy

AFTER LOSING HIS 1983 MAYORAL campaign, Billy resigned his circuit court judgeship in order to stand on the other side of the bench and represent clients. That's where the money was. And that's where he thought he'd be able to make the sort of impact he was hungry for. Within three years, he was the top lawyer in the city, taking big criminal cases that mattered. Cases that made the papers. Cases the city paid attention to, and paid money to make go away. For the next three decades Billy was one of the most visible legal figures in Baltimore and made millions of dollars, building one of the top legal firms in the country, Murphy, Falcon, and Murphy. The firm focused on multiple aspects of law—criminal cases, civil litigation, athlete representation—but he also took on some of the highest-profile cases involving police brutality, including the case that helped put him on the map, that of Albert Mosley.

On June 25, 2003, Albert Mosley, a middle-aged African American man on probation, was out drinking. On his way home he was stopped by police, who arrested him for public drunkenness and brought him to the Western District police station. While in the station, he apparently became unruly and got into a shouting match with officers. While Mosley was still handcuffed, the officers slammed him into a cement wall, and, unable to break his own fall, he landed face-first on the cement floor. He lay there bleeding and unable to move for forty-five minutes until finally he was given medical attention and taken to the hospital. As a result of his injuries Mosley was paralyzed from the waist down and barely able to move his arms. Billy became his counsel, and after a contentious and public battle that lasted two years, the City was found culpable and Albert Mosley received a $44 million payment, at the time the largest payout in a police brutality case in Baltimore history. When he was interviewed right after the verdict, Mosley said, "I didn't believe there was justice in the world until yesterday. I've finally seen justice and I thank God for my attorney Billy Murphy. I am indebted to him for the rest of my life."

This case made Billy the first stop for people who had complaints against the police department. Billy built an entire lane of his business on this premise, and Baltimore provided a pipeline of cases that kept his firm busy.

Billy realized soon after agreeing to represent Freddie's family that this case was going to be different. When he first saw Freddie at the hospital, he had been in a coma for four days, kept alive only by a respirator. Repeatedly shaking his head as he looked at the fragile man in the hospital bed, Billy asked himself the question the community was asking: How had Freddie come to be lying there with an almost fully severed spine, when just days ago he'd been perfectly fine?

Even after the video of the screaming man went viral, it seemed that no city leader was concerned with finding out. Soon after taking the case, Billy picked up his phone and called the mayor, Stephanie Rawlings-Blake. He assumed she knew about the case already, and he just wanted Baltimore's chief executive to know about the storm that was headed her way. When Billy had the mayor on the phone, he said, "Hey, Madam Mayor, we need to talk about my new client, Freddie Gray." There was a pause on the other end of the phone before the mayor's answer: "Who's that?"

Billy shuttled between the hospital and the neighborhood where Freddie had taken his final steps, trying to get details. Billy understood that what made this case different was not just the fact that it involved police—that wasn't new either to Billy or to the community—but how willing people were to talk. Usually people don't want to talk, particularly in cases involving violence, for fear of retribution, worried that they might be putting themselves or their family in harm's way by cooperating. Billy was used to the blank stares people would give to him when he would ask if they'd seen anything regarding a case he was working on. But Billy was startled by how different things were with this case. Older women came up to him, almost cheering him on: "Get 'em, Billy." He was approached by young mothers in nurses' uniforms returning from work. Young men with gold-fronted teeth. Grandparents dressed up walking with their grandchildren dressed down. Pulling his arm, wanting to show him exactly where things had happened. Billy took notes, hurriedly moving his pen across the page.

Billy knew about Freddie's rap sheet. Between 2007 and 2015, Freddie Gray had been arrested seventeen times. Charged with crimes ranging from illegal gambling, trespassing, and possession of marijuana to malicious destruction of property and fourth-degree burglary, Freddie was a very familiar figure to the police in the neighborhood. But that wasn't the Freddie the neighborhood was describing to Billy. Outrage and heartache poured from the lips of the West Baltimore residents that Billy interviewed. Freddie had been the kid that everyone in the neighborhood knew and liked. "Not that kid." "Not Freddie." "Freddie never bothered anybody." "Freddie always has nice things to say." "Freddie just goes 'bout his business." "Why him?" Unlike other cases in which Billy struggled to get any piece of information, in Freddie's case the streets were talking. And the streets wanted justice.

Greg

G REG'S FATHER RETURNED TO GET him and his sisters from Preston Street when he was seven, and life got better.

They moved to Calhoun Street, in Sandtown, and life got much better. When his dad had left, he had begun building a life he'd be able to share with his children. He even met a woman, Denoris Gilmore, who would become a stable female presence in Greg's life.

Greg senior went out of his way to make the new home special for his son. He knew that with the move, he was taking Greg away from a community that he loved. Both he and his son were boxing fans—and Greg junior used to visit the legendary Mack Lewis Boxing Gym on the East Side—so in outfitting his son's new room in the basement, Greg senior made sure it had a speed bag, a punching bag, and a weight bench. He got him a tricked-out bike, too, that the boy would ride back over to East Baltimore when he was homesick.

Despite his new life, Greg craved his past. Until Gerlena disappeared, little Greg had been a momma's boy. For a long time, no one would tell him why she was no longer living with them. His sisters and father still treated him like a baby, even though he'd been forced to grow up so fast. He didn't like that they didn't explain things to him, as if he wouldn't understand, despite all that he'd seen. What his dad and older sisters didn't realize was that while they thought they were protecting him, leaving him in the dark meant that he was forced to deal with his emotions without any context to explain them. So one day, in third grade, he left Dallas F. Nicholas Sr. Elementary in the middle of the day and went looking for answers himself. He walked up and down Greenmount Avenue on an unsuccessful mission to find his mother. When his father found out that he'd left school, he finally told the boy the truth. "Look, son," Greg senior said, "your mother's on drugs. She ain't in her right mind right now."

After he left his mother's house in 2001, he saw her just one time. He remembered sitting with his dad and sister Cameal outside of school, waiting for his sister Serena to get out of tutoring, when Gerlena rode by in the passenger seat of a Jeep Wrangler with a man little Greg didn't know and she screamed out the window, "I love you." The Jeep never stopped. He wouldn't see her again until 2008, when he visited her in prison at the Maryland Correctional Institution for Women in Jessup on Mother's Day.

Despite the distractions of his home life, Greg excelled in elementary school. He always sought out positions of authority, from line leader to safety monitor, and was named a Ben Carson Scholar. His principal decided he wouldn't go anywhere but the best middle school; she pulled some strings, and Greg was off to Roland Park Elementary/Middle, a school in a wealthy North Baltimore neighborhood. The public school was tucked in among a number of the city's private schools, including Gilman, which educated children from the city's wealthy families, like the Angelos family.

It wasn't too far into his sixth-grade year that Greg got put out. He just couldn't adjust. This was the first time that he had been around large numbers of white people in school—white teachers, white facilitators. Though the school was only across town, he felt like he was in a different world, out of place. In a way it was easier for him to play the part of the bad guy, because it felt like he was expected to be. There were plenty of black kids at Roland Park, but they didn't share his experiences growing up in a Baltimore ghetto. Maybe he was projecting, but his discomfort morphed into contempt. Looking back, he would come to realize that he just didn't do well in predominantly white settings.

His father was disappointed when Greg transferred from Roland Park to Robert Poole Junior High School, which was not a good school—in fact, the school would close a few years later because of its persistent problems—but he used it as a way to teach his son a lesson. "See, now you get to be around all of your homeboys like you wanted to," he said to Greg.

Robert Poole was dangerous. Not the kind of danger Greg was used to, with neighborhood spats between the kids from Greenmount Avenue and those from Barclay Street or Lanvale Street and the occasional fistfight, but the life-threatening kind of dangerous. Kids were getting banked, and it was at Robert Poole that he first started seeing knives and guns introduced to fights. It was also at Robert Poole that he first saw a sawed-off shotgun. By seventh grade, he was carrying a box cutter to school.

Still, Greg excelled. That was in part because of the Franciscan Youth Center (FYC), which offered mentoring as well as summer and after-school programs in the city that Greg and his sisters had participated in for much of their childhood. When a couple of years later the family moved to Garrett Avenue, in the Coldstream Homestead Montebello neighborhood, the kids' connection with FYC meant that they could attend Waverly Elementary/Middle School, which was one of the schools FYC was partnering with and which was better than their local school, Stadium.

Greg loved eighth grade at Waverly. He was going to school with all black kids and was taught by all black teachers—all of whom lived in his neighborhood. He was in an accelerated academics program, scored high on standardized tests, and took Algebra 1. He had graduated from playing rec basketball to an AAU team, and loved the sport. So when it came time to choose a high school, it was clear where Greg was headed: Baltimore Polytechnic Institute, his first choice, and one of the best high schools in the city.

Nick

Nᴉᴄᴋ ꜱᴀᴛ ᴜᴘ ɪɴ ʙᴇᴅ, staring at the television in disbelief. His wife, who was the newly elected Baltimore state's attorney, sat next to him, intently reading the briefing materials on her lap. They had always been clear about keeping a sort of "ethics wall" between their work, as two of the most powerful people in Baltimore with very different job responsibilities— one to make the laws, the other to enforce them—slept next to each other at night.

Though he worried it would disturb his wife, Nick turned the volume up slightly to catch every word. The mayor, in a beige blouse and black suit, was giving a speech. Behind her stood the Baltimore head of the NAACP, Congressman Elijah Cummings, some members of Freddie Gray's family, and other municipal leaders including Councilman Brandon Scott. Scott was a rising star in the Maryland Democratic Party and someone the mayor saw as a protégé, but his district was on the other side of Baltimore from where the direct impacts of the unrest had occurred.

Today the mayor struck a very different tone than she had

in her press conference the day before, where just hours after the violence at the baseball stadium, standing together with some of the city's most influential pastors, imams, and community leaders, she had urged reconciliation and understanding, trying to get all sides to appreciate the positions of the others. During the Saturday press conference she had also made a statement that had gone viral and made her fodder for news outlets and a scapegoat for people who blamed the violence on opportunism more than anything else. She'd said, "I have worked closely with police to make sure protesters were able to exercise their right to free speech. It's a very delicate balancing act where we try to make sure that they were protected from the cars and the other things that were going on. We also gave those who wished to destroy space to do that as well. And we work very hard to keep that balance and to put ourselves in the best position to deescalate and that is what you saw."

Nick understood how the language she'd used on Saturday had been misinterpreted and spun to make her look bad. He felt that what she'd really meant hadn't been as bad as the statement had come out sounding. But he was also frustrated by City Hall's response to the entire incident. It wasn't what the mayor said; it was what she wasn't saying, whom she and other leaders weren't talking to. It wasn't the coordination; it was the lack of coordination.

Nick's neighborhood stood strangely quiet. Usually from his small three-bedroom rowhouse, which sat minutes away from where Freddie would be buried the next morning, he could hear the occasional siren and other accents of the street. But tonight there was nothing. He and Marilyn had just put their daughters to bed; the girls slept in the room next door, largely unaware of what was going on around their parents.

His glasses firmly placed on his face, Nick listened to every word that the mayor said on television that Sunday evening. She passionately reminded her community, the community of her birth, that Freddie was going to be buried the next day and that the family was calling for a pause to the protests. She assured the community that the wheels of justice were moving and accountability would be had. She reminded Baltimore that City Hall had a full awareness of what was going on in the area and was prepared to respond.

Nick, the City Council member who represented Freddie Gray's district, winced. Her words reminded him that he hadn't heard from City Hall in days.

He leaned over, looked at his wife, and took her hand. "Let's say a prayer for the city."

MONDAY, APRIL 27

Greg

G REG WOKE UP LATE MONDAY morning groggy and unsettled. It was the alcohol and the weed daze, but also
something more ominous. Across town, thousands were de-
scending on New Shiloh Baptist Church for Freddie Gray's
funeral. After a weekend of chaos surrounding his death, today
was supposed to help Freddie rest in peace.

Greg had taken the day off from work to renew his driver's
license, and he planned to leave for the DMV as soon as his
uncle dropped off his last week's pay. He enjoyed working with
Marlon in the home improvement business. It was the kind of
work that's brutal on the body but good for the soul. When he
was working in someone's house, he'd always have conversations with the people who lived there that he'd never have had
in the more impersonal setting of an office. Whether it was
Section 8 housing or million-dollar mansions, he always felt
connected to the people who lived there—like their equal. He
never felt dismissed as a young guy; rather, he was treated as
someone who had valuable life experience. It was legitimizing

for him to be able to have these conversations and be able to hold his own.

While he waited for his uncle, Greg strolled around the neighborhood, looking for some conversation. He wanted to take the temperature of the city and gauge how everyone was recovering from the weekend. Some said they'd heard that tensions were still reverberating downtown, and the answers to his questions confirmed that the worst was still yet to come. Neighbor after neighbor declined his invitation to go downtown to where the action was brewing, and most had some variation of the same response: "Don't you take your ass out there."

Greg decided to go somewhere that kept him out of trouble. The tall, sturdy young man climbed the hill to his most sacred place, the basketball court behind Coldstream Elementary and Middle School. That's where he often went to clear his head, pounding rubber against pavement for hours until dusk settled over the skyline and the city's stars, the lights of the Transamerica Tower, the Legg Mason Tower, and the Pandora building. The facade of urban splendor masked the realities of his life in Baltimore: poverty, drugs, violence.

Greg always turned to basketball in times of tumult and turmoil, and April 27 was brewing with both. Over the last three days the anger and fear that had been swelling in the city had begun to spill over, peaceful marches turning into rage-filled protests with violence and destruction. Greg knew from his own life that rage didn't subside in a matter of hours.

He'd tried to put on a good face for the last three years, telling himself that the Coldstream basketball court was just as good as the gleaming court of a college. He had earned a full scholarship to college while playing for Poly, where he had become a basketball star almost overnight, it seemed. He didn't play ball for Poly his ninth-grade year. He was still working at the FYC as an assistant group leader, overseeing its after-school program, mentoring the younger kids, the ones in kindergarten, first grade, second grade. He helped them with homework, fixed lunches, cleaned up the building. He'd continued playing AAU ball regularly, though.

By the end of freshman year, Greg had made a lot of friends, including Poly basketball players he'd play pickup games with, and it was clear it was time for him to hoop for real. The next fall he tried out for varsity and made it.

Poly's team, the Engineers, wasn't known for winning until Sam Brand came along. The tall, lanky white man arrived in Greg's junior year and shook everything up. He told them how to play, how to understand the game, how to win. Sam and the boys started on a journey together to be respected in the city. And soon they started climbing together. In one breakout game from 2012, number one Dunbar scraped out a narrow 58–51 win over number thirteen Poly. The Engineers, *The Baltimore Sun* reported, got a game-high seventeen points from senior Greg Butler.

Sam and Greg formed what would become a lasting bond. Sam let Greg miss practices to work in his uncle's home improvement business. Greg needed to make money to help his single father, who still struggled with the bills, and also to pay for the ancillary costs of attending a largely affluent high school: team trips, new clothes, new shoes.

Sam knew that Greg was special. He'd always promised Greg, whom he constantly praised as brilliant, that if he pushed himself, it would pay off. And when he discovered that it wasn't really true, at least not for a black kid from Baltimore, Sam was devastated.

Sam was also a math teacher, and a year after Greg graduated, he became the source of one of Sam's most formidable lessons. For six months, Sam led his math class in a project investigating a recurring issue that he saw beginning to affect his student athletes. They were taking rigorous honors and advanced placement courses that qualified for extra "quality points," but their weighted GPAs were coming up short. The students researched the policy, called other school districts, compared their syllabi and transcripts to their friends' in surrounding school districts, and calculated and recalculated GPAs to compare the grading systems of the city and neighboring county. They presented their findings to a stunned Baltimore City school board in April 2014, crystallizing the point with a real-life example of how this policy had already shattered dreams.

A star basketball player, the students told the board, had been taking rigorous courses all four years of high school and was relying on certain "quality points" awarded for honors and advanced placement courses to boost his GPA and lock in his qualification for the NCAA. He had a scholarship waiting for him at Saint Leo University in Florida. But it was discovered after his GPA fell short that the Baltimore City school system awarded its students only a fraction of the quality points awarded by schools in neighboring Baltimore County and every other suburb in the state. Greg Butler, who had graduated two years earlier, had missed the GPA cutoff to qualify for the NCAA by a fraction of a point.

Tawanda

TAWANDA SAT AND WATCHED AS the men in suits smiled, cackled, and shook hands. Poverty pimps, she called them, the ones who showed up in their fancy suits and said all the right things to capitalize on black pain—politicians, ambulance-chasing lawyers, so-called community leaders. She recognized a few who, two years earlier, had conveniently cared about Tyrone when cameras were around but then disappeared as soon as the TV crews went elsewhere. But the pain had stayed with Tawanda.

It was April 27, and Tawanda had come to New Shiloh to pay her respects to Freddie's family, along with the rest of Baltimore. His funeral was one of the biggest events of the year, where the oppressed and oppressors gathered to memorialize a casualty of their divisions.

She stared at his mother, whom she'd marched with just days ago. Tawanda had told her that day to keep hope alive. Guilt swelled in Tawanda as she looked at Gloria's face, showing so much agony. Maybe she should have told Gloria the truth: there is little hope for justice when those who are charged with enforcing it kill your loved ones.

She narrowed her eyes at all of the police officers who'd had the nerve to show their faces at the church for Freddie's funeral—like the punchline of a sick joke. She'd heard this joke before. After Tyrone died, the police had been everywhere, it seemed—in the neighborhood, around her house, even at the funeral home when she went to see his body for the first time. Shortly after he died, the police department sent a well-known black lieutenant colonel from the Western District to ask if Tyrone had any "preexisting conditions." Right before the funeral, they sent another to help fry chicken. *That's what they do,* she thought, *send out the house Negro to comfort the black family. The one they feel can connect to the grieving family, pray, talk about how the violence is destroying our communities, how hard it is to be a black man in America.* She knew the police did this to convince the families that they understood, that they were the good guys; they thought making fried chicken—the ultimate comfort food—was the way to do that. Tawanda told the lieutenant colonel she'd rather fry chicken with her brother.

Five days before Tyrone died, he and Tawanda had attended services at New Antioch Baptist Church, where he'd been baptized in 2011, and a member since 2012. That Sunday, July 14, was not even twenty-four hours after a Florida jury found George Zimmerman not guilty of shooting a teenager walking through his neighborhood eating Skittles. Zimmerman had thought the teenager looked suspicious, wrestled the boy to the ground, shot him, and admitted it, and twelve people said it was justified.

The verdict and its significance weighed heavily on the nation, and on New Antioch's Bishop Orlando Wilson. "I want y'all to be careful because it seems like black lives don't matter," he said.

"Sis, my body can't stop shaking. It felt like the pastor was talking just to me," Tyrone said to Tawanda after the service ended. "All y'all disappeared and it was just me and him in the church. I feel scared. I feel like he was talking to me, telling me to be careful."

"Oh my God, brother, be careful," she replied. Then she changed the subject to something more comfortable, a topic they addressed every Sunday afternoon. "Where we going for Sunday dinner?" she asked.

Weeks later Tyrone returned to church, no longer alive, and this time he was the subject of the sermon. Seeing her brother lying in a box had been unreal. It felt to Tawanda like she was in there with him, like all the breath had left her body, her spirit hovering above the congregation. She couldn't remember who'd been there, what the pastor had said, whether she'd cried.

A year after his death, *The Baltimore Sun* published witness and police testimony that would offer Tawanda some of the only details she'd ever have about her brother's final moments. The accounts described how police pulled him over in her 1999 Mercedes-Benz for a traffic violation and what they saw as "furtive movements" in the car. How they badgered the woman who was driving with him, accusing her of having drugs, though they found none in the car. How Tyrone was perturbed by being pulled over, put up a fuss, and then surrendered after fighting off officers, saying, "'You got me, you got me, stop hitting me." How he broke away and ran, yelling, "Help" and "Trayvon Martin." How police said they saw a bulge of what they believed was drugs in his sock, and a witness overhearing him speak of a "measly" amount. How one officer kicked West in the head, another beat him with a baton. How a group of spectators pleaded with them to stop.

Now she grew angrier and angrier with each speaker who took to the lectern at Freddie's funeral, to preach to the crowd as if they really knew the pain that Freddie's family, her family, was feeling.

Everybody wants to talk, but where were y'all when my family was telling y'all all this stuff for two years straight? she thought. *They could've avoided Freddie's death if they'd just listened.*

As far as she was concerned, the whole damn lot of them had blood on their hands.

Billy

THE PREPARATION FOR FREDDIE'S FUNERAL was more deliberate and coordinated than anything else that had happened that week. Every element of the schedule of events for the funeral had meaning. The family insisted on the funeral being in the community where Freddie lived and had last been seen. They wanted his service to be in the heart of West Baltimore, walking distance for people who really knew Freddie so that they could mourn the young man they loved. But it also had to be at a church big enough to hold a funeral that many in Baltimore knew would be nothing like anything they had ever seen. Everything had to be well thought out. The positioning of the cameras and media. The songs they'd sing. Where people would sit. Who was acknowledged. Who was not. Who would pay for it. Who would speak and when.

Baltimore's power elite knew that camera crews from around the world would be capturing every facial expression and reaction, and so political angling masked in altruism was everywhere during the ceremony. Mayor Stephanie Rawlings-Blake sat in the front, surrounded by throngs of people who yearned for her job and understood that this was a defining moment for the city, one that voters would remember at the next election.

Black funerals sometimes take on a celebratory tenor. Not just a mournful farewell, but a joyful commemoration of a life well-lived. An acknowledgment of a homegoing, a reunification with family members who passed before. An entrance into heaven to join a God ready to welcome you in. No more pain. No more heartache. No more suffering. At these funerals, tears and shouting blend into joyful praise. Their origins shade all the way back to the first introductions of Africans to what became the United States, when elements of traditional African beliefs and practices merged with elements of Christian orthodoxy. When life was spent in captivity and brutal labor, homegoing to a place of peace and rest—a place of glory— was a cause for gratitude. Resting in peace was earned.

That was not the case this morning at Freddie's funeral. Here the presiding feeling was not one of celebration. It was one of intolerance for the system that had ended a young man's life. People were not there to celebrate the life of Freddie. His life had been tragic. They wanted to share their collective feelings of frustration and maybe hear a vision for a direction forward.

When Billy entered the sanctuary he gestured to his longtime advisor, Ron Owens, who had helped to organize the funeral, and pulled him aside.

"I want to speak," Billy said. "I think I should say something."

Ron knew the schedule was already packed, and he'd already had to tell dozens of powerful ministers no. The Rev. Jesse Jackson was set to speak later in the funeral. Ron began to shake his head—but then he looked in Billy's eyes and realized this was not a request. Billy was going to speak that morning.

Billy's turn came, and he got up in front of the congregation. Before he opened his mouth, he paused and looked out over the crowd, letting the moment sink in. Billy knew the city didn't need a political speech; what it needed was a social justice sermon. Billy's normally controlled pace was replaced by a minister's cadence, complete with breaks for the crowd to ring in with "Amen!" and "Tell 'em!" Billy knew that many in that crowd weren't regular churchgoers, but it didn't matter whether or not they knew Jesus. They knew police brutality. They knew the cries of mothers when they received word that their sons were lost. He wanted to take the moment not to mourn the weak but to blame the powerful.

He worked the crowd like they were a jury, and Billy was determined to win this case, as he had won so many before. He leaned on Proverbs 11: *The Lord detests dishonest scales, but accurate weights find favor with him. Wealth is worthless in the days of wrath, but righteousness delivers from the death. Whoever derides their neighbor has no sense. But the one who has understanding holds their tongue. Be sure of this, the wicked will not go unpunished. But those who are righteous will go free.*

Billy sat down to raucous applause. He closed his eyes and smiled, responding to the spontaneous acknowledgment from a city that needed to hear his words. He hadn't been on the program. He hadn't had anything prepared. The plan when he woke up that morning had been to attend Freddie's funeral just to pay his respects. But when he walked into the church that day, something happened. He saw the family, still burdened by the weight of their newfound notoriety. He saw Freddie lying in the casket and the well-wishers surrounding his body. But, most important, he saw the crowd and the cameras. This was not a normal funeral. The world was watching. And Billy was not going to lose his moment.

The crowd leaped and cheered. His jury pool of two thousand people came to taste the flavor of justice. And Billy rested his case.

Greg

Looking down over downtown, Greg felt that he and everyone like him needed to get into survival mode, this time maybe even prepare for war.

For too long, it seemed, the warriors had been avoiding the inevitable. Greg considered himself one of them. The police hadn't started messing with him until he'd started to get some size. It had been back in high school, which wasn't too long ago but felt like a lifetime. He'd started hanging out downtown in the summertime, when everybody showed up with friends from their neighborhood, and that was when he had his first interaction with the police. He'd been down at the Inner Harbor with about six other friends, big dudes who played football, and they were leaving the twenty-four-hour Subway. They were walking up the street and saw their bus, the one that would take them back to Belair Edison, and they started running to catch it. All of a sudden ten cops came out of nowhere and pushed them up against the wall of the 7-Eleven on Baltimore Street.

From their profanity-laced rants, Greg recalled, the cops

thought he and his friends were running from a fight, that they had just jumped somebody. The cops were pulling out all the tricks: cursing them out for no reason, pushing up against them.

Greg had seen his father deal with police before, and Greg senior wasn't a coward. Once Greg senior was being followed while driving, and he'd pulled over to the side of the road, hopped out of the car, and just started yelling: "The hell you following me for?" So Greg was prepared. He wasn't going to go down without a fight.

One particular white officer was going off, cussing up a storm. Greg was sitting on the pavement, giving it right back to him. But he was also confused: *What's going on? Why are you talking to me like this?*

In front of nine other cops, including the high-ranking ones in the white shirts, that officer picked Greg up by his shirt and, all in one motion, slammed Greg against the wall and punched him in the throat. Greg was taller than the cop, and he remembered looking up at the sky, waiting for the cop to take his fist off his throat so he could punch the cop and run. One of the white shirts must've sensed it, because he approached Greg and said through clenched teeth: "I wish the hell you would."

From then on, it became normal to be harassed by police. He got pulled over driving around his neighborhood, snatched out of the car, hemmed up. Before he was even asked for his license or told what he'd done to be pulled over, it was "Where the weed at? Where the coke at? Where the dope at? Where the guns at?" He quickly learned to just let them search so that they'd let him get back in the car. It was a simple equation: comply = get back home.

He was repeatedly harassed in front of one particular building in his neighborhood, on Kirk Avenue. He eventually learned that it housed the police's Internal Affairs Division. It made him laugh to think how many times he'd been harassed in front of the building that he was supposed to report such incidents to. It was just another example of how disconnected communities are from the institutions that are supposed to protect and serve them, but which aren't really there to protect or serve at all.

That April Monday, the day of Freddie Gray's funeral, Greg kept thinking he should turn around and head back down the hill toward home. But he kept standing there, his head full. He remembered a phrase his uncle would repeat to him when they would have their "deep talks"—about wars, about the civil rights movement: "Where will you be when the revolution comes?"

As his eyes panned the city from his perch, he was looking at a familiar backdrop, but it was a view he hadn't ever fully taken in before. Then his gaze fell on the helicopters he could hear growling in the distance. They weren't like the ones that occasionally roared through the hood at night, police helicopters hard-heartedly known as "ghetto birds," shining their bright lights through people's windows, looking for black men like slave masters used to do with their torches.

These helicopters, four of them, hovered. And they all circled around a cloud of smoke rising from a single point. It wasn't an area he'd ever paid much attention to. It wasn't distinguishable like the rest of the city was from that vantage point, by a landmark or a corporate stamp.

Greg realized that for the first time he was on the Coldstream basketball court without a basketball. For the first time Greg realized that from the basketball court, you could see West Baltimore.

Tawanda

MIKE BROWN. WALTER SCOTT. TAMIR RICE. Laquan McDonald. Eric Garner. Freddie Gray. Before all of them, there was Tyrone West.

Yet Tawanda's brother was probably the least-known among the lineup of victims whose deaths had spurred marches throughout the nation over the last few years as the Black Lives Matter movement emerged. That wasn't fair. But Tawanda had given up on fair a long time ago—from the moment they'd assigned Tyrone the name "John Doe" even though he had a driver's license on him with all of his identifying information.

It was five days before they would let her see her brother's body. The police officer who had been dropping in and out of her home did try to prepare her: "You might have to have a closed casket," he said.

In the days since his death hit the news, community activists and city representatives had done what they do best: show up to help when it was too late. A community activist said he'd help pay for the funeral, and that would be $10,000 that she could keep in her daughter's college fund and one less thing to worry about, so she gratefully accepted it. The gift never came through, after the family learned that the money would come with people dictating details of how they grieved, down to where they held a candlelight vigil.

Tawanda had called and asked the funeral home not to pump her brother full of embalming fluid until she saw what was left of him after his encounter with the police. The funeral director said something about germs, but she didn't care. She and her brother shared the same blood.

In the car on the way over to Brown, she prayed for God to give her strength to see what was left of Tyrone. She expected that he'd be bruised, maybe even disfigured.

"I didn't know your brother, but he looks pretty good," the funeral home lady told Tawanda before leading her to the preparation room where her brother's body awaited.

What she saw stopped her heart.

"No, no!" she screamed.

Tyrone was smiling.

Tawanda knew two things: that her brother had not been smiling when he died handcuffed on the hot pavement, and that someone had reconstructed his face to make it seem that for the past five days he had been resting in peace. She also knew that she couldn't understand how the body she viewed, her brother's soulless corpse, could be defined by anybody as looking good. In addition to boot prints on the side of his head, on his neck, and all over his body, she stared at the elongated scars on his torso from the baton beatings that she could only describe as looking like train tracks. He had chunks of skin cut away from his face. She placed the burgundy sheet back over his body, knowing the images she just witnessed would haunt her forever.

That's when she realized that she couldn't rely on any of those jokers in expensive suits, paying their respects to the family as if they cared. That's when she knew she was going to have to take matters into her own hands, even if it meant taking on the very people in power who were supposed to protect her and her family.

Before Tyrone's cold body was claimed, police were putting the finishing touches on a narrative they'd started working on when they pulled him down to the pavement by his dreadlocks on Kitmore Road. But the black men who died just like him helped Tawanda put together a narrative of her own over the years. That was the moment the police yelled at him not to resist, but he wasn't resisting; he was fighting for his life, just like Trayvon. They attacked him because they were "scared" of his size, like with Mike. Because they instantly treated him as a threat, like Tamir. Because he was an unarmed black man, driving his car and minding his own business, like Walter. Because he was acting "erratically," like Laquan. So he had to be manhandled, like Anthony. And he died because for some reason he couldn't breathe, like Eric. From the moment her brother was stopped, the police had been building a case not just for killing him but for assassinating his character.

At first they claimed he'd been in poor health. "Did your brother have a heart condition?" the detective asked when he came to the house.

Then they painted him as a liar. "Mr. West handed me his driver's license and it had a fake weight and height," another officer told her.

And a drug user: "Come on, you gonna arrest me for these

measly bags?" the police recalled him asking when they had him on the ground.

Tyrone had just had a physical, and he was healthy. He loved the ladies, so he kept his towering frame in shape, looking buff. He exercised by walking every morning, sometimes from East Baltimore to West, and he'd get in some extra walking as he helped his grandmother exercise. As a Christian, he took seriously that his body was a temple. Tawanda only knew her brother to smoke a little weed here and there, and like every other part of the investigation conducted by the city, the toxicology result was suspicious: it found cocaine in his urine, but no drugs in his bloodstream. Besides, he could've used every drug on the market, but that's not a capital crime warranting summary execution by cops on the street.

And "measly"? Tawanda had never heard her brother use that word in his life.

Tawanda knew that if it had been her, if she'd died and police said they found her drunk with a pack of Newports on the highway, Tyrone would have smelled a lie. She'd had two Coors in her entire life and gotten pissy drunk, and she hadn't touched the stuff since then. She's terrified of highways, and on her way to her job at a suburban school she allows twenty extra minutes so that she can take a route through city streets and avoid the highway.

They lie about the dead because the dead can't talk, Tawanda thought.

But Tyrone talked to her.

About a year after her brother's death, Tawanda had tossed and turned in her bed one night, asking Tyrone and God for a sign. Her brother had been the subject of many prayers since the day he was killed, and though he was buried, she was convinced he wasn't resting, so neither could she.

She knew he had not found peace because she could feel him stirring everywhere. Sometimes she could still hear his voice: *Sis, don't let me go out like that with no heart attack. You know I'm healthy.*

They had always had a spiritual sibling connection, starting when they were little. They would have silent conversations just by looking at each other, an unspoken language like the kind they say twins sometimes have. Each could sense when the other was in trouble, too. If somebody was messing with her, before she could even call his name, he was coming around the corner. Every day, the guilt of not having been able to have his back the way he'd always done for her was too much to bear.

The night she'd been unable to sleep, she'd heard a loud crash, and she got up from her bed to tiptoe throughout the house, worrying that she was going to have to confront an intruder. But her fiancé was still sound asleep, and the kids were motionless in their room.

When she returned to her room, she looked down at her bed, and there was a photo of Tyrone staring back up at her. She knew the photo: it had been affixed to the bedroom mirror. It wouldn't even come off with Windex when she cleaned it.

The clock struck three. She only had two and a half more hours before she had to be up, get dressed, and get the kids ready to go to school, so she gave up on sleep and turned to a pastime she had engaged in a lot in recent months. She flicked the remote on the TV and turned to the Investigation Discovery channel, which featured true-crime programs—the ones where police go back and retrace their steps, or some new piece of evidence turns up, and at the end someone cries out, "I knew it!"

It was the top of the hour, just in time for a new episode of one of the shows she'd been watching. She loved when she could track a case from the beginning. She almost always solved the case before the police did.

This episode was about a decade-old case of a young kid whose death had been ruled an accidental drowning, but his mother remained unconvinced. *Yup, families always know*, Tawanda thought. The mortician on the television described how the case was extraordinary, how after all of these years the little boy's tissue was intact, as if he'd been waiting for his mother to find out the truth: he had been poisoned.

You gotta be kidding me, Tawanda thought, sitting up slightly.

When the new test results came back, the mother on the television ended up filing charges against her sister. It turned out that the boy's aunt had been molesting him. They'd found his body in a creek down by the sister's house one day, though nobody ever understood how he'd gotten there. With that revelation, things started to make sense for the mother—how her son had always cried when she dropped him off at her sister's before she went to work.

Tawanda sat in her bed, breathless, as she realized what Tyrone was trying to tell her. The only way she was going to unearth the truth was to unearth her brother's body.

Partee

BY MONDAY, PARTEE THOUGHT THE worst was over. Or at least his history on the force and his history in Baltimore made him hope that was the case. He thought that maybe with the events of Saturday the protesters had gotten the raw anger out of their system. They'd marched, they'd busted up cars, they'd tried to stop the baseball game; it had been ugly, but everyone survived. A reckoning had come and then passed. Now it was time to move forward.

But there were still loose ends to deal with. At the eight o'clock meeting at police headquarters Monday morning, the police commissioner laid out what to expect in the days ahead. The briefing was focused on social media, where the department had gleaned some intel about something that might happen at Mondawmin Mall. The word that they were seeing used on social media was "purge."

The term had originated with the 2013 horror flick *The Purge*, which depicted a dystopian American future in which for one day each year, from sunset to sunrise, all crime was legal. Murder, rape, manslaughter, robbery, it didn't matter—

this was a time for people to "purge," to release their pent-up frustrations, satisfy revenge, and unleash their id with no inhibitions. Partee was familiar with the film. But from the contexts in which the term was appearing in social media, Partee knew that this wasn't just a bunch of kids looking for an excuse to enjoy some chaos and destruction. They were trying to tell the rest of the world something. This was a social commentary.

Even so, Partee didn't take the social media rumors too seriously. Mondawmin didn't seem like a hot spot. It had the usual stores and restaurants, and because of the nearby Metro station, it also served as a transportation hub, with thousands passing through it to catch buses and trains each day. It was an ordinary place, a place for Baltimoreans—in contrast to the Inner Harbor, which was Baltimore's representation to the world.

After the meeting, his commanding officer pulled him aside. She wanted him to go to Mondawmin. "I need a strong command presence there," she told him.

He rarely ever protested an assignment, but he made it clear he didn't want to go to Mondawmin. He wanted to be at his usual post at the Inner Harbor. But eventually he relented, figuring Mondawmin was close enough to his district in case anything serious popped off.

It was late morning when Partee and his unit posted up in the mall's parking lot, which faced Frederick Douglass High School across Gwynns Falls Parkway. His team that day consisted of twenty-one officers, a lieutenant, and three sergeants. He did not initially think it was overkill to have that many officers at Mondawmin Mall. He took a couple of loops around the perimeter of the mall and saw nothing and nobody unusual— pretty much what he had figured. He breathed a sigh of relief.

Jenny

JENNY WAS SHATTERED AND EXHAUSTED as she headed to work on Monday, the day of Freddie Gray's funeral. It was bright and sunny, but there was a dark cloud hanging over the city. It had been there since Saturday night, the night the storm descended on the city. She couldn't shake the image of the protesters' hardened faces just inches away from the police officers'. The people had finally been empowered to face their overseers and tell them they'd had enough. But she knew the police, she passed them every day, and she knew one thing they didn't appreciate was being made to look foolish or weak.

It was around eleven that morning when she heard the word "purge" on the radio. She wrote it down as part of her notes because it rang a bell. She'd heard it about eight months earlier, on an August day in the courthouse. Eighteen-year-old Mike Brown had been gunned down in Ferguson, Missouri. All over the country, including in Baltimore, protests were being planned. Law enforcement in Baltimore was buzzing that their city could blow up, and rumors were starting to fly that the violence might be planned. Jenny couldn't tell if it was just hype. She knew the running joke in Baltimore that whenever there was bad weather, everyone tried to convince their boss to shut down the office for the day and let everybody go home; sheriff's deputies at the courthouse pulled it all the time. But reports of such severe impending rainstorms or snowstorms or windstorms were almost always just hype.

That August day in 2014, though, a storm had actually come.

Jenny had been planning to join the Baltimore protesters who were going to march for Mike Brown, and she had started making rounds in the courthouse to recruit her colleagues to go with her. One of the sheriff's deputies discouraged her, saying, "You shouldn't go, Ms. Egan, because there's going to be a purge," he said.

"What is a purge?" she asked.

He turned his phone around to show her a posting from the Fraternal Order of Police listserv that featured images of the ominous masks from the 2013 movie plus a date in August 2014 and a time. Until that April Monday in 2015, that was the only time she'd ever heard anything about a "purge," and it was from the mouth of a law enforcement officer.

Greg

GREG FELT HE HAD BEEN saved from the 2002 firebombing on Preston Street, and years later it still haunted him. He imagines his experience is like that of people who were running late to meetings in the Twin Towers when the planes hit on 9/11. In the years after, Greg struggled to make sense of what felt like a brush with death. He figured there must be a reason why, just days after the fire, he saw his ninth birthday; he assumed there was some purpose he had to put his life to for every new year he was able to see from that day forth. Maybe it was survivor's guilt; he didn't know about that. Just another input challenging his mental health as he worked to navigate life. When soldiers return from combat, we stress mental health services and counseling, rightly spending time and resources helping our servicemembers process how they can return to a life of peace and progress when they are still mentally existing in a framework of war and fatalism. But for our young people who have to process unimaginable pain, we somehow think they are better equipped to deal with it in isolation. We ask our soldiers to remember and process. We ask our young people to forget and move on. We underestimate how difficult it is to do well in school when the trauma of violence and poverty takes up the lion's share of your thinking and emotions and the last thing on your mind that day is how you will do on your biology test.

Greg felt an obligation to take advantage of the opportunity he'd been given and that many of his dear friends, including the Dawsons, had been robbed of: to reach his potential. But he understood that in Baltimore City, a young black man's potential was limited by structural factors. He went to the best springboard he could, Poly, and even there he felt the societal deck stacked against him. He and other black students were at the mercy of a school system that didn't seem to care about whether or not its children could see themselves in what they were learning. He knew for a fact that he was one of the smartest students at Poly, but his grades in no way reflected that. Looking back, he realized it was because he couldn't relate to much inside the textbooks he was given. The white children he sat next to could relate. The system had been created for them. If you're of a certain race and can't look inside a history book and see where you started, it's hard to fathom where you can go. He believed that's why it had been so easy for him to see himself in the NBA, where 70 to 80 percent of the players are black.

On this Monday, he stood on the Coldstream basketball court having not even reached half of his potential. He was a shadow of what he could have been. He felt that he had followed the path laid before him, to focus on school and basketball, and it just didn't work out.

Depending on the day, he vacillated between anger and resignation about his lost opportunity. But he settled into his job at his uncle's home improvement company, where he'd worked all through high school, and he enrolled in community college in a nearby suburb. His father, who had been helping him pay for his education, lost his job, and Greg fell behind on his tuition. Even then, Greg kept taking classes until he was barred from doing so. His dream of college died because of an unpaid $2,958 tuition bill.

Here he was three years later, standing at the top of a hill overlooking the city, his hands empty, his eyes wide open. He felt a stirring, one he hadn't felt in a while. And he saw a sign. He saw the pain, the frustration, the hatred visible and rising, culminating in a dark cloud billowing over the west side of the city.

He decided to follow the spiraling smoke.

Partee

PARTEE HAD PEOPLE ON STANDBY, sitting in police vans, waiting. They were staged on the other side of the mall, away from the Metro entrance. He wanted to keep them out of the way because he didn't want even the insinuation that his guys might have started to stir things up.

Partee met up with members of the school police force, another independent security unit, who patrolled near Frederick Douglass High School every day. He figured they knew the kids, dealt with them every day, so they could steer the crowds when they let out of school in the next hour. He and his guys would monitor and provide backup if need be.

A little before dismissal time, the crowds of kids started pouring out of Douglass, crossing the bridge toward the bus hub at the mall—a scene that played out every day. But today they were met by a group of protesters who had been lingering around waiting for them to walk out of school at three o'clock, as promised in the "purge" postings. Partee began to notice a merging of the groups, the high school kids in their school uniform of orange polos and khaki pants mixing with the protesters in street clothes. His head swiveled as he saw yet another group turning a street corner and joining the mass of people already there. This group looked to be younger, middle school students, and they were wearing a different school uniform.

The merged groups began walking toward the officers with their arms raised, chanting the familiar refrain: "Hands up. Don't shoot. Hands up. Don't shoot." The chant was what protesters in Ferguson had adopted after the shooting death of Michael Brown. A shared pain was being expressed through a shared slogan.

Partee's antennae went up. *What is this? Why are they doing this? There's no reason to do this.* He had hoped today would be a quiet day of reflection, that it would look more like the relative calm of Sunday instead of the chaos of Saturday.

He headed toward the area where the school police force had gathered, looking for answers, but his fellow officers seemed just as confused.

"I have no clue what's going on," one told him. "I don't know what this is."

"Hands up. Don't shoot," chanted the group.

Partee thought it was time to act.

The vans stocked with riot equipment revved up their engines, and officers started to gear up—everyone but Partee. Even as the others began to suit up, Partee tried to convince himself that it was just a precaution.

Then a bottle flew. Soon a hailstorm of rocks and bottles enveloped the police.

Partee had the main van parked a few rows from the walkway that led from the Mondawmin Mall to Douglass. There were two other vans staged on the opposite side of the mall.

The officers stayed in the vans during the initial chants, but as the crowd got larger, Partee called the officers out of the vans.

Partee arranged for a wall of officers, now fully geared up, to move in on the crowd pelting them. As the line of officers marched forward, Partee saw the kids break ranks, and some scurried toward a 7-Eleven that was across the street, about one block northwest of the bus loop at the mall. Inside, he could see that the business owners had armed themselves with cans of pepper spray, which they were using to fend off potential looters.

Partee set his sights on one kid he'd identified as the instigator. He told a group of his officers, rookies who had recently graduated from the academy, that he wanted that one. He needed just one in custody to feel a sense of control. But no sooner had they identified the kid than he slipped out of their grasp, back into the chaos.

The rocks were coming in fast and hard by this point. Shields were starting to splinter; chunks of hard plastic were breaking off. The officers watched one by one as their only protection disintegrated in their hands.

The officers were now looking around like, *What are we gonna do now?* Partee got on his radio to request support and additional equipment: "Hey, get me more shields. Get me more equipment. Get me more stuff up here."

One of the big unanswered questions from the day surrounds the decision to shut down public transportation at Mondawmin. There are sixteen bus, train, or metro stops at Mondawmin Mall, making it one of the true transportation hubs in a city not known for its public transportation assets. A disruption at Mondawmin has citywide consequences, not to mention that most of the students at Frederick Douglass High

School and many other area schools rely on public transportation to get to and from school. The shutdown at Mondawmin trapped the children there at just the moment the police would've preferred they disperse.

Partee was furious when he heard about the shutdown, but had no idea who'd made the call. Chaos was rippling around him, and whoever had issued the order clearly hadn't thought it through. The crowds were swelling with kids who couldn't get on their bus to go home.

He watched a large group of kids coming northbound on Reisterstown Road from his line of officers with their damaged shields. Some of the kids had rocks or bottles in their hands. *Somehow we've become target practice for these kids*, he thought. With that, he'd had enough. He began barking commands to his officers: "Push forward!" The officers started marching across the street to confront the kids.

The order ended up being consequential—mostly for his officers. It trapped some of them on a side street, and as a result they were surrounded on all sides by pelting rocks and debris. One officer had his head busted. Frustration overtook the force; Partee heard later that some of them lost their cool and decided to defend themselves by throwing rocks back at the protesters, including children.

As the officers began moving, the young people headed away from them, up a hill, and they began to split off into alleys that led off the Gwynns Falls Parkway. Partee figured that if the officers kept pushing the kids farther and farther away, he would push them out of the core area, which would force them to disperse. He didn't realize that he was also pushing them toward another major intersection, the corner of North and Pennsylvania Avenues.

Jenny

AFTER SPENDING THE MORNING IN court hearings Jenny headed over to the main public defender's office on St. Paul Street around lunchtime, shortly after the courthouse joined the rolling closures in the city. At the public defender's office, the band of attorneys, which would eventually become the Baltimore Action Legal Team, had once again gathered to offer their assistance.

When she arrived, the visiting lawyers were discussing their concerns about what would happen to the kids being released from school around the Mondawmin Mall. But because none of them knew the area, they had no idea how to get there. Jenny volunteered to lead the way.

Jenny drove them to the Mondawmin neighborhood and parked at Druid Hill Park. She and three other legal observers walked up the block toward Gwynns Falls Parkway and the mall.

As the group walked, Jenny saw rocks all over the ground. Helicopters hovered overhead. TV crews were there with their cameras and microphones. She could see a line of police still pushing crowds of kids south, away from the mall. And she didn't see a single bus moving.

That day, Jenny also started her Twitter account, the only way that she could monitor the uprising. Social media would become a powerful platform for her to defend the city's youth in the court of public opinion.

In a Facebook post, she wrote one of the first counternarratives to emerge after a press conference where the police commissioner would blame the city's students for starting the battle at Mondawmin. "I think these were youth coming out of the high school and they thought it was cute to throw cinder blocks at the police department," Commissioner Anthony Batts said. In response, Jenny wrote:

Mondawmin transit stop is where all the buses in B'more converge. Kids in B'more don't have zoned schools and so they take 2–3 buses and go to school all over the city. At 3 PM there are always 500 kids at Mondawmin. Every day. Those kids weren't rioting, they were trying to get home. Community members say police arrived in riot gear as early as 1:30 to "prepare." Kids in large part stayed away, kids who were there were confronted by police in riot gear, tapping batons against shields. Then they stopped running buses—stranding everyone in the midst of a police attack. This was a riot, this was police provocation. I personally saw 12 gauge rubber bullets. They were shot at children. Tear gas. Fired at kids.

Greg

GREG MADE HIS WAY FROM his home on Kirk Avenue along Montpelier Street, looking for recruits to accompany him on his pilgrimage. "Anybody trying to go downtown?" he would ask. Each time the answer was no.

Greg didn't understand why no one shared his sense of urgency. The city was rising up at last. This is what they'd all sat around and talked about—the day when everything could change. Just like Baltimore to sit by when it was time to stand up, Greg thought wearily.

Finally he ran into a neighbor, White Boy Chris, who said he was heading in the direction of the Penn North neighborhood. Chris understood the gravity of what was unfolding in the city and was on his way to his storage unit to prepare. Even though he was seen as a harmless junkie in the hood, Chris seemed to realize that today he was about as vulnerable as he'd ever be as a white man. Today, unlike most days in Baltimore, black lives were the ones that mattered. So Chris was headed to retrieve his arsenal, just in case he had to fight for his own.

Greg hopped in the car with Chris and his girlfriend and rode with them to the storage unit. There he told them he was going to walk the rest of the way and get as close as he could to the source of the smoke. Before Greg got out of the car, White Boy Chris told him to be safe, to make sure that he was covered and protected. Greg had a pocketknife, which he'd always carried and never used, and a ski mask, which he'd picked up at Chris's unit. But Chris thought that wasn't proper gear for a warrior. He dug around in his gear, lifted something up, and said to Greg, "This is what you need."

He handed Greg a gas mask.

Nick

"SORRY, COUNCILMAN, WE HAVE TO push you a little further out. We are still following new developments at a school in the area. We plan on getting to you as soon as possible." The distinctive nasally voice Nick was hearing in his earpiece belonged to CNN's Wolf Blitzer.

"No worries," Nick responded into the microphone clipped to his tie.

Over the past couple of weeks Nick had given dozens of interviews, serving as one of the voices of Baltimore in the wake of the Gray incident. In countless languages and in countless accents, he'd heard the words "Baltimore," "Freddie Gray," "police," and "protests." He and a handful of City Council members and community leaders had become steady media go-tos when the press was looking for someone to help their global audiences comprehend how everything had seemingly unraveled so quickly.

But Nick challenged the premise that it had all happened suddenly. He saw that this outrage had been brewing for a generation. Only now was the world finally paying attention.

Today Nick was on the air to talk about the funeral. Hours earlier he'd been sitting in a pew at New Shiloh Baptist Church in the same three-piece suit he had on now.

Nick had stopped counting the funerals of community members he had attended. Many of them were for young black males from the district he represented. In that year, there were 344 homicides in a city of 622,000, and close to 65 percent of those bodies fell in West Baltimore. But this funeral was different, in part because it was one of the few that he attended alone—his wife was still investigating whether this funeral was the result of a crime.

Nick recalled how when Mayor Stephanie Rawlings-Blake had been announced as the next speaker, there had been a muted reaction from the crowd in the church—a silent protest of her job performance, he thought. Their reaction to her was in sharp contrast to the welcome they'd given to Rawlings-Blake's predecessor in the mayor's office, Sheila Dixon, who'd been removed from office in 2010 after being convicted on one misdemeanor count related to misappropriating gift cards intended for the poor. The applause when she was introduced showed that despite her fall from political grace, her political capital in the community was real.

As Nick waited for further word from the producer, he knew that what he wanted to convey to Blitzer and the CNN audience was that this funeral was about much more than Freddie Gray. It was about much more than justice. It was even about much more than Baltimore.

Just then Nick heard the sound of helicopters overhead. On any given day you could hear a helicopter now and again, but today there seemed to be an urgency to the sound that was abnormal for a midday Monday in West Baltimore. And it sounded as though all of the choppers were heading in the same direction—toward Nick's district.

The producer came back on. "Councilman, I am so sorry. Something is really going on at the school. We are not going to be able to get to you today. We will be back in touch."

Partee

"ALL RIGHT, WHAT ARE WE gonna do?" said Police Commissioner Anthony Batts, directing his gaze toward Partee. Batts, a PhD and former chief of police in Oakland, had spent much of his life and professional career in California, but he had been running the Baltimore City police department, the eighth-largest municipal police force in America (for the nation's twenty-fifth-largest city), since 2012, brought in by the new mayor, who'd felt pressured to hire someone from the outside with a history of department reform. In a city that is 65 percent African American, it also helped that he was black.

Batts was known to be no-nonsense and hands-on, and he frequently spoke about his experience in complex situations. As a young officer, he'd witnessed Los Angeles burn after the acquittal of the officers who were caught on video brutally beating Rodney King after a traffic stop. During his tenure as the chief of police in Long Beach, California, homicides decreased by 45 percent. He was the police chief in Oakland when a twenty-two-year-old man named Oscar Grant was pulled from a train in the early morning hours by a transit officer, who forced him to the ground and subsequently shot him in the back. Protests and rioting ensued, and Batts was widely praised for the way he handled the situation. When he came to Baltimore he promised to reduce crime as long as he received the necessary operational authority and support.

Partee had always respected Batts, and he appreciated how difficult it had been for this black man to rise through the ranks in an organization that was not initially built for inclusion of African Americans. Batts was also active in the community, which the rank-and-file officers liked because it made their jobs easier.

But now Batts's clean-shaven head and scowling face loomed directly in front of Partee as the two met in front of Mondawmin Mall.

Maybe it was the way Batts looked at him, the five-foot-nine police commissioner craning his neck to stare up at the six-foot-four Partee. Partee had just seen one of his officers rushed to the hospital with blood pouring down his face. Another officer had been hit in the groin with a cinder block. A third officer had had her ankle broken. Partee was feeling the weight of all this.

Batts asked why Partee didn't have his helmet on, a fair question from a chief to a commander during a time of unrest. Partee responded tightly that he had given it to a member of his team who had neither a helmet nor a riot shield and was "shaking in her boots."

The most recent revision of Baltimore's policy for riot control had been put in place in 1977. There was no curriculum on riot control at the police academy. In 2014, all Baltimore police officers had received three hours of training on crowd and protest control, mainly consisting of watching videos. The scenarios they had examined were mostly nonviolent protests. They had been instructed on how to allow space for peaceable assembly. So the training was of virtually no use in managing this upheaval, which had turned bloody and violent. Partee had to operate on instinct. And now his boss, who had been through the worst kind of civic violence in other jurisdictions, was asking him why he had been cursing on the radio.

An angry Partee stepped up to Batts, his face inches away from the chief's. "Either I'm in charge or you are in charge," he told him. "If you're in charge, go ahead and tell them what to do. If not, leave me the hell alone! I've got work to do." Their eyes locked for a few more seconds, each waiting for the other to make the next move. Finally Partee turned and walked away.

Greg

WHITE BOY CHRIS DROPPED GREG off at West Twenty-eighth and Sisson and Greg took a thirty-minute walk, landing near Upton–Avenue Market station, right near Shake & Bake. From blocks away, the intersection of North and Pennsylvania Avenues was nearly impossible to see, sunk in a fog of smoke and pepper spray. But Greg could hear it. The sirens, the shouting, the choppers overhead, cops on a loudspeaker asking people to go home. A police car was on fire; so were a van and a CVS. As he neared the crossroads, he came across a bike lying on the sidewalk. He decided to borrow it.

As he knifed the bike into the smoky intersection, Greg found himself in a crowd that looked like nothing he'd ever seen. So many Baltimores were converging. He rode in slow circles, passing kids in school uniforms, lines of city police, clergy members, gang members, Nation of Islam brothers, longtime activists, newly minted protesters, legal observers in bright yellow hats, and out-of-town cops dressed for what looked like battle. Some cops were operating an LRAD (long-range acoustic device), a sound cannon whose power was multiples stronger than the traditional loudspeaker. It was usually used for nonlethal crowd control, scattering protesters with its crazy-making, high-pitched shrieks, but it was used in other applications as well, such as deterring wildlife from congregating near airport runways, nuclear power facilities, and industrial plants.

In this weird, hazy, liminal space, none of the usual rules applied. Police stood motionless as people ran into stores and emerged not just with liquor, pills, and phones but toilet paper, Q-tips, and baby formula. Westside guys who'd normally steer clear of Greg dapped him up like they were old friends. Leaders of the Crips, Bloods, and Black Guerrilla Family nodded to each other on their way to scare looters out of mom-and-pop shops. Folks who'd stolen water, schnapps, and cigarettes were sharing them with strangers. As Greg rode around, the burning, rock-throwing, and epithet-shouting, everything he had seen on TV earlier, were starting to subside. Now a new wave of people was arriving. Most, like him, had come because they'd seen something historic unfolding. Not that everyone came for just the spectacle or the significance. People broke into one store and didn't just loot it—they dragged out the Asian proprietor, beat him, and left him lying in a gutter. Police deployed pepper foggers that left protesters clutching their eyes, searching for milk or Maalox from a crew of volunteer medics.

Jenny

J ENNY RAN BACK TO HER car as the other legal observers began jogging to keep up with the moving crowds. As she headed down North Avenue toward Pennsylvania Avenue, it became clear when she'd arrived at ground zero: she saw armored vehicles headed her way, and people streaming out of stores, arms full of rolls of toilet paper and diapers they hadn't paid for.

She parked and ran into the daze that was the scene at Penn North, where she saw that flames had begun to dance in the air. She ran back and forth for what seemed like hours, taking notes. Her phone had been dead for three hours and she had gotten separated from her observing partner, Justin Hansford, a law professor who had also worked in Ferguson, who had bad asthma and couldn't handle the smoke. So she had no way to communicate with anyone to let them know that she was safe.

At one point she dropped her phone. In the next second she saw a boy pick it up. They made eye contact, and she pleaded, "No, no, no, no, no. It's mine. It's mine." The phone was useless right at that moment, but she couldn't bear the thought of all that would be lost when the boy ran off with it.

He stared her right in the eyes, slightly amused.

"I know," he said. "And you thought I wasn't going to give it back to you."

Jenny's stomach dropped and her eyes burned with tears.

He was right. That's exactly what she'd thought. Her mind had betrayed her heart, and he'd called her on it.

Why would I assume he wasn't going to give it back to me? she thought later, after the events of the day were over. *We were both out there for the same thing and for the same reason.* Every day she stood before judges to fight such prejudgments and prejudices, especially involving kids. Yet in that fleeting moment, she was guilty of the very thing she had been fighting against.

As much as she loved the city where she now lived, she always felt the guilt of escaping the reality that its natives have suffered—poverty so intense, so hard, so deliberate that it was suffocating. She considered herself a kind of opportunist in this tragically magical city—she'd been able to buy a nice house, in a predominantly white neighborhood in a majority-black city, for a reasonable price, because she had a decent job and she could figure out how to work within the system of real estate agents and mortgages and tax breaks and everything else that's involved in buying a house. No matter how much she fought to address the frustrations of the people she lived among, she knew one thing would always separate her from those she defended: privilege.

She'd been drawn to the city after living for a while in Washington, DC, a city whose elitism had made her feel as uncomfortable as she'd been at Barnard years earlier. She'd had a fellowship working for the National Women's Law Center in DC, after completing the University of Michigan Law

School, and she kept finding herself in Baltimore for concerts or art shows. The city was quirky, like her, and she felt at home there. She asked her wife, who worked in the District of Columbia in federal policy, if they could move to Baltimore. She said maybe in five years. Not long after that the city of Baltimore posted a job for a juvenile public defender, and within two days Jenny got the job. They were living in Baltimore within five months.

What the world saw as chaos that day, Jenny saw as redemption. The same kids throwing bottles were the same ones who were stripped of their dignity on every other day.

For years nobody believed their stories of their interactions with the police. They told of how, starting around fourth grade, when they got some size, the police would pull them off their bikes, call them criminals, pull up on them in their cars as they walked home from school, line them up on the sidewalks, and grab their balls in front of their friends. The cops would walk behind them wielding those big wooden nightsticks, the ones that became so infamous for beating folks that they were mementos for cops who retired from the department. But on this day the power players had become mere props in the kids' drama. The police merely stood there as kids popped wheelies in defiance. Neighbors were taking pictures in front of the wall of helmets and shields like they were a backdrop at the club. That day Jenny felt the joy circulating in streets where there was often so much pain. It reinforced for Jenny that she was on the right side of history. The boy reminded her how fragile that standing can be.

Nick

Nick's black Mercedes E-Class raced through the streets from West Baltimore to City Hall, where his City Council colleagues had decided to hold their regularly scheduled meeting. By the time he hit North Avenue, though, he knew it was anything but a regular day.

He navigated streets littered with cars that had been suddenly abandoned; one of them was on fire. An MTA van sat burning, emitting black smoke that clouded the otherwise blue sky. His eyes fell on kids openly busting windows in parked vehicles, some with T-shirts tied around their faces and others unmasked. As he watched in disbelief, he made eye contact with some of the young people. Nick wondered what they saw when they looked at him. Did they see a council member who had been fighting for their communities? Did they see a city leader who was advocating for more funding for schools and community centers? Or did they just see another suit, another guy who was part of a system—protecting that system, benefiting from that system—that had screwed them over? Nick had never been afraid of Baltimore, but this wasn't the Balti-

more he recognized. And he knew it would not recognize him
as anything more than another guy who was part of the system.

His tires screeched as he sped down North Avenue, heading
downtown. He pulled into his parking spot at City Hall and
sprinted to the fifth floor, where the fifteen City Council members had their offices. Having just seen the burning devastation of West Baltimore, Nick felt a surrealistic sense being in
City Hall, where people were conducting business as usual. He
checked his phone. No calls from the mayor. No calls from the
council president.

As Nick was preparing to walk through the doors of the
council president's office to update him on what was going on,
his phone finally rang. The ominous "unknown" flashed on his
caller ID, meaning it was either someone really important or
not important at all. He answered the call and discovered that
it was the White House. For a brief moment a shocked Nick
stood completely still, puzzled about how they had even gotten his cellphone number, but then he remembered it was the
White House. He was on the line with the pinnacle of power at
the exact moment when he had never felt more powerless.

A senior member of Valerie Jarrett's team was on the other
end of the phone. Jarrett, a longtime trusted friend of the
Obamas and an accomplished businesswoman in her own right,
served as a senior advisor to the president. The White House
staffer on the phone with Nick skipped the pleasantries and
got right to the point.

"Councilman, we are monitoring what's going on up there
closely. We are trying to figure out if we need to support
what's going on up there."

Nick could hardly believe his ears. *If?*

He launched into a searing account of what he'd just seen.

He didn't only talk about the damage to buildings and vehicles. He told the staffer about the eyes of the young people. About the mixture of pent-up fear and anger that was now exploding over West Baltimore. Nick pulled no punches. He felt like he didn't have to. More importantly, he felt like he couldn't. He had never seen the city of his birth in so much pain.

After Nick finished talking, there was a pause on the other end. Then the voice coming from Washington, DC, told Nick that this was news to them, because the city had told them they had it under control.

Greg

WITH HIS BORROWED GAS MASK on, Greg could get close to the police line, and he easily ducked the bottles that were flying through the air. He weaved in and out of the space that separated the protesters and police, realizing that this middle ground was a stage and that the media were out in droves. He realized that the police were behind him and his people were in front of him—the way it should be. He took the opportunity to yell out to the people, tell them that they had the power, and that it came in the form of the masses who had taken to the streets that day.

Then he threw his fist into the air.

Cameras clicked from all around. It felt good. Good enough that he kept at it, posing for a series of photos that would later become iconic images of Baltimore's riots that spread from North Avenue to Britain to Venezuela, as the man in the gas mask became the face of a revolution.

Just a few minutes later, he would cement his place in Baltimore's history when he spotted a fire hose.

CVS is the largest pharmacy chain in the United States, and

its parent company ranked as the seventh-largest corporation in the Fortune 500. So the burning CVS store at the corner of North and Pennsylvania stood as a monument of the day, the symbol of victory for people who had finally been able to take out their frustration on corporate America and all that it represented.

The fire trucks arrived to extinguish the fire as Greg and other protesters had begun to mill about, wondering what was next. It seemed that they were losing their direction. Greg had used all the tools he had at his disposal to rally the crowd— the mask, the bike, his voice. He reached into his pocket and pulled out the one tool he had left, his pocketknife. In an instant he cut the fire hose, and water began to spray from the puncture. Seconds later, he came back and stabbed a second hole.

Greg was an instant hero. Strangers hugged and high-fived him. He did a little dance as he hopped on his bike. He was a leader.

When Greg challenged the Nation of Islam brothers who were trying to get protesters to comply with police demands to move, strangers stopped, gathered, listened, passed him looted bottles of alcohol, and patted him on the back. He felt like the man he always thought he'd be: someone with something to say, somebody worth listening to, someone who believed that actions spoke louder than words.

Jenny

THE STREET MEDICS WERE EVERYWHERE, at least twenty of them, maybe more, people Jenny had never seen before and would never see again. The pepper spray had saturated Pennsylvania Avenue, and the volunteers were weaving in and out of the smoke from the burning CVS as they attended to people up and down the street. The smoke thickened. But Jenny couldn't leave. Not now.

She watched as firefighters arrived at a hydrant and police began to help uncoil a big fire hose. She felt her stomach tighten. Of course she knew that firefighters fought fires, and that fire crews would need to put out the conflagrations around the intersection. But she also knew from the history books that when a *police officer* had a fire hose, it was for one reason: to hose down protesters. Scared, her adrenaline pumping, she braced for the powerful shower that she thought was very likely. She saw a CNN crew nearby and felt a fleeting sense of satisfaction that at least the hosing would be broadcast.

The police began hitting their shields, screaming, "Arrgh, arrgh, arrgh, arrgh, arrgh!" They started circling the protesters like sharks. It didn't make sense. Jenny had been corralled before, but had never seen anything like this. They grunted, ran toward protesters, and pinned people against walls, but then wouldn't arrest them.

God, they have no idea what they're doing, she thought. They had lost control, which made her even more convinced that the police were going to hose down the protesters.

The fire hose lay on the street. Fire sirens wailed in the background.

A towering figure moved toward the hose, a knife gleaming in his hand. In one motion he swooped down and punctured the hose, then kept walking. In that moment, Jenny felt protected; the man in the gas mask had saved her.

Partee

PARTEE WAS EXHAUSTED. HE STOOD at Penn North as a coalition of officers from around the state tried to bring some semblance of order and calm to a situation that was in complete disarray. He was now in his fifteenth hour on the job, and the protesters seemed to be more emboldened while the officers just seemed more frustrated.

He was hungry, too. The only meal he'd had that day had come when some of his officers went to the Royal Farms convenience store to grab some chicken and pizza. A few hours ago a police van had come to bring the officers on the scene water and snacks—but when the van stopped, its doors opened, the officers inside dumped two cases of water and the food on the median strip, slammed the doors, and zoomed off. He knew that the officers in the van were what he and his fellow street cops called "house cats"—administrators who sit behind desks, file the paperwork, ask questions, and have few answers—and he could understand that they didn't want to be there; he didn't want to be there, either. Still, what they did pissed him off. *You just gonna throw the food on the ground like that like we're a bunch of dogs?* he thought.

Partee looked at the chaos on the street. The officers had been told repeatedly that they were not to do anything about the looting and lawlessness going on around them. "Don't engage," headquarters told them.

All around him were abandoned houses. Less than fifty years ago the city's population had been nearly a million. Now it had dropped by a third, and what had once been warm, lively residences were decrepit shells. The tired police officers sitting on their steps looked on as fires burned and stores were looted, their eyes asking, *What are we supposed to do?* He had no answer for them.

For Partee the final straw came later that night, when he was in a line with his other officers trying to keep protesters from interfering with the firefighters who were putting out the blazes engulfing cars and buildings. Looking over his right shoulder, he saw a well-built young man standing in front of the skirmish line with a gas mask on. The young man pulled out a knife.

Partee reached to his hip and pulled out his taser, intending to stop the young man with the knife from doing whatever he was thinking of doing with it.

But a deputy commissioner, Dean Palmere, grabbed his arm. "If you tase him, I am going to take that from you," he said, staring Partee dead in the eye.

Partee's hand froze. He was shocked, but at the same time he understood why Palmere was saying that.

Partee wished that everyone who screamed about how excessive the police were, how they overreacted, could stand in his shoes at that very moment. When people are getting shot in their community, they want the police there. But now the police were watching people break the law right in front of them, and they couldn't engage. People seemed to want it both ways, he thought—lawbreakers could engage the police and that was okay, but if the police tried to engage, they were abusive.

Feeling defeated, Partee looked back at the young man with the knife as he punctured the fire hose. The crowd cheered. Partee just turned his head in the other direction.

Billy

WHEN BILLY ARRIVED BACK AT New Shiloh Baptist Church Monday evening, he had no idea he was walking into a civil war within the civil rights movement.

He had been asked to come back and make a few comments by New Shiloh's pastor, Harold Carter Jr., a third-generation preacher in Baltimore and head of one of the most powerful congregations in the city. Since 1996 Carter had led this church that thousands of Marylanders called home, having taken over the helm from his father, Harold Carter Sr. The community knew and deeply respected the Carter name and what the family represented and contributed to the city; many were able to tell personal stories about how the Carters had helped get them a job, pay for school, or pay for the burial of a loved one. But that evening the enormous church was full of pastors, community leaders, and community members, all arguing.

It had started when the Rev. Frank Reid, one of the leading voices in the city, invited members of the community who were gang affiliated to New Shiloh. Bloods in red and Crips in blue crowded into the church, upset because of the rumor going around that the gangs had agreed to work together to kill cops. This narrative was being pushed by the police department and had been echoed by city leaders, including many of the community leaders in attendance. The gang leaders were furious, not only because the rumor wasn't true but also because it was being used to blame the gang members for the violence of the night and to justify intensifying the policing of them. "They are lying on us! And y'all are pushing it and allowing it!"

Tensions stayed high as those present debated how the community should respond. Some of the gang-affiliated members resented being labeled as "gangbangers" or "thugs," arguing that they were some of the ones out there trying to restore peace that night. Community members pushed back: the community isn't safe, they said, not just because of aggressive policing but also because of the actions of the young people sporting red or blue bandannas.

Billy hadn't been prepared to do more than just say a few words that night, as Carter had suggested, but on the spot he decided to use the moment to speak on a topic he'd wanted to bring up earlier at the funeral but ultimately chose not to: the history of policing and why the disputes happening in the church that night were part of a larger, deliberate strategy of destruction by separation that had been carved out generations ago.

Billy's "make a few comments" became an off-the-cuff, forty-five-minute lecture about how policing in the United States was as old as the country's founding. The growth in population had created a greater level of social unrest, and the introduction of enslaved people as a core driver of economic status introduced the need for policing units that could help masters better control their investments. This led to the creation of slave patrols in South Carolina in the 1700s. They quickly spread and eventually became the first publicly funded policing forces in the nation. Their primary functions included searches of slave lodges, keeping enslaved people off roadways, and disrupting organized meetings of those enslaved. They were known for their brutality and lack of accountability, and remained in place long after the Civil War ended.

The audience listened raptly as Billy gave an extemporaneous account of the foundation that the Baltimore police force, and every other police force in the United States, stood on. He concluded, "My brothers, I represent a family whose heart is broken today. Let's be clear about who broke it."

As Billy returned to his seat, he placed his hand on the forearm of Rick Shipley, Freddie's stepfather. Billy whispered in his ear that the congregation would like to hear from him, even just a few words. He hesitated, as following Billy Murphy is an unenviable task. But it was more than that. While he understood Billy's point about historic suppression of blacks and police brutality, only hours earlier he had watched the casket lid close on his son's embalmed body, knowing the last thing Freddie's now-closed eyes had seen.

Rick reluctantly eased himself up from the pew and slowly moved to the front of the sanctuary as the group rose in thunderous applause. Rick was the left-behind. The survivor. The heartbroken. Freddie's remaining voice.

Rick reached the front of the room, fingers fidgeting with the wedding ring on his other hand. He cleared his throat and began to speak, his fatigued voice barely audible but his message resonant. "I am not a historian, but I am a father who lost his son and buried him today." He paused, and there was silence. Ministers and politicians leaned in. People who were live-tweeting the events of the day put down their cellphones.

Rick spoke about the pain his family was feeling, not only around laying their son to rest but around the uprising that Freddie's homegoing had triggered. He spoke about watching leaders argue with one another, about watching young kids fight each other. "Why are we killing each other?" he asked. He spoke for five minutes in a stream of consciousness, his words striking directly into the heart of the room. Before he collapsed back into his seat, his final words to those assembled were, "We are all we've got."

Nick

Nick had just left the City Council meeting, where he had been shocked to find out that the unrest taking place just a few blocks away in West Baltimore was not on the council's agenda. Everything in the council chambers was business as usual. At the end of the meeting Nick got up and made an honest plea to the council, to those observing the council meeting, and to anyone who could hear him to pray for his district. He detailed what he had seen on his way to the meeting just a short time before. Those assembled listened to him speak, then reluctantly applauded. Nick rushed out of the meeting determined to take his message to the streets.

"Every man in Baltimore City, if you care about this city, come meet us to take back our community. We need to let these young brothers know that this is wrong and they are loved." That was the tweet Nick sent out to his ten thousand followers, urging them to meet him and a group of influential ministers and take to the streets of West Baltimore.

After sending his tweet, he departed to go to the meeting at New Shiloh. He exchanged pleasantries with the other civic and religious leaders there, who earlier that day had assembled in the church for Freddie Gray's homegoing and to pray for his family but were all in astonishment that this was what the day had devolved into. Now they found themselves praying for the city and a swath of its citizenry who felt that prayers were not enough.

Then the march that Nick had called for began. A group of a few dozen leaders, Nick in the middle of them, began walking down North Avenue singing spirituals, and as they walked the group grew to well over a hundred, including Congressman Elijah Cummings and the Rev. Donté Hickman, a Baltimore product who now led the influential Southern Baptist Church. Everyday citizens of Baltimore were coming up to the group and asking for personal prayers, as if these leaders who had locked arms and were moving en masse could expedite requests to God. And the pastors would cluster around the individual making the request, asking God to watch over that person and calling for Jehovah to provide grace and mercy.

After the march ended, the ministers and community leaders returned to the church, feeling pleased they had walked the streets and prayed over the city. They knew their work was hardly done, of course, but maybe their group contribution for the night was. One minister from East Baltimore commented to Nick that he had no idea that West Baltimore had blocks that were so dilapidated.

Morgan State University associate professor Lawrence Brown famously described the pattern of racial hypersegregation in Baltimore as the "Black Butterfly." The concentration of blacks in the western and eastern parts of the city, with whites in an L-shaped pattern that runs roughly north–south between those two concentrations and then down to the southeast, looks much like the shape of a butterfly with outspread wings. If you took the map of Baltimore and superimposed that butterfly image over it, you'd have a map of where opportunity lives or dies. Where the butterfly wings are, covering East and West Baltimore, they block light and hope. Transportation assets, lending facilities, and policing standards all differed depending on whether or not your neighborhood fell under the shadow of those wings. Outside the butterfly's wings, highways were built to provide access to downtown. Under the wings, highways were built over neighborhoods, causing displacement. Outside the butterfly's wings were concentrated large numbers of traditional banks, financial institutions that met an entrepreneur's aspirations with opportunities. Under the butterfly's wings, check-cashing storefronts, payday lending outfits, and pawn shops reigned. Outside the butterfly's wings were quality grocery stores that sold food to nourish both mind and body, fuel for a full day and a full life. Under the butterfly's wings was a landscape of food deserts and small corner stores selling unhealthy processed food.

That was why Nick was surprised to hear the minister talk about East Baltimore as if it were better off. As if West Baltimore corners didn't mirror those in East Baltimore. As if Baltimore's apartheid created bigger losers in West Baltimore than in East Baltimore.

Back at New Shiloh, some of the most powerful black leaders in the city sat in the pews, telling stories about what they'd seen that day and what they would do next. They shared stories of people who were drunk on the streets. They laughed at the fact that on the same block you could see a burning car at one end and at the other someone dancing to Michael Jackson songs on top of a vehicle, singing off-key.

Nick's day had been long, but he wasn't satisfied. He still wore the same outfit he'd had on at Freddie's funeral earlier, a

three-piece gray suit with a solid black tie and a black hand-
kerchief peeking out from the left breast pocket, but his white
shirt had taken on a dingy aspect, and the fabric of the suit
reeked of sweat and smoke. All of a sudden the praying, the
marching, the linking of arms felt trite and wildly insufficient.
Nick's thoughts turned from the people who'd joined their
march to the people who had not approached them—the ones
who stood looking on, wearing "the mask that grins and lies,"
as the poet Paul Laurence Dunbar said. Now Nick realized his
day wasn't over yet. He had to go back out there and actually
engage the young men who watched from afar. They were his
constituents, too. They were kids whose childhoods mirrored
his, but their future hopes seemed much dimmer at the moment. Nick needed to go tell them they were loved. He needed
to go tell them to get off the streets so that this night didn't
get worse. He needed to go tell them that when the National
Guard got involved, nothing positive would come to a young
black man lingering on the street. For a night like tonight,
with so much at stake, marching through the streets and singing songs would be incommensurate.

Standing up, Nick called on the others still at the church to
join him and head back out to Penn and North. He shared his
plan to further engage the young men in the hope they would
go home and not damage anything else or get arrested. A
dozen of the younger men agreed to join him—some of them
community leaders, some ministers, some campaign volunteers for Nick, none older than forty.

When they got back to Penn North, the hour was edging
closer to midnight and the crowds were still large. The pain in
the streets was still palpable, and the anger on the faces of the
young men was real.

Nick had been scared at points in his life. Growing up in

Baltimore, he had experienced violence. He had a flashback to when he'd been robbed in Baltimore when he was home from college, lying with his forehead on the pavement while the barrel of a gun touched the back of his skull. Another flashback to when he and his sister had walked into a Tyrone's Chicken in the middle of a robbery. But while he had tasted fear before, it had never been as intense as what he experienced on the dark streets of Penn North that evening.

As Nick stood there with twelve other men, a small fraction of the number he had walked with hours before, buildings were still burning and there were no police present. He saw people running in and out of stores but no store owners. His eyes widened at the scene of anarchy. He thought about his two little girls at home and his wife, to whom he had not spoken all night, and pushed down the fear. Then he approached the young black men and asked them to go home. He told them nothing was going on out there that they needed to stick around for. He told them he wanted them to survive the night. Some blew Nick off; some listened.

Then Nick's eyes locked on a young man, maybe sixteen years old, a younger version of himself. Sweat glistened on the young man's forehead. Nick asked him to go home and stay safe.

The young man's face changed suddenly, almost as if Nick had flipped a switch that he did not mean to. The young man reached down and lifted up the hem of his T-shirt, exposing a gun.

He looked straight into Nick's eyes and said, "No justice, no peace. I ain't going nowhere."

Greg

O F ALL THE PLANS GREG had that day, ending up in the 7-Eleven wasn't one of them. But there he was, in the middle of one turned upside down from a night of looting, searching for cigarettes. It was there that the police caught him.

Greg didn't want to be extracted from the streets. That was where the people had the power. Once he was behind bars, he'd be back in the grip of the system.

And then he saw the police van.

Not today, Greg thought. *I can't get in that van.*

So he struggled, figuring that if they had a plan to do something in the van, he was going to make it hard for them. He ran and got a few blocks away, outrunning the officer who was on foot. The police officer who ultimately caught him was on a bike.

They put the cuffs on real tight, and Greg climbed into the back of the van and sat on a bench with a few other arrestees. The woman who was driving the van was actually kind of nice, though she got all preachy, telling him that he needed to get his life together.

You haven't the slightest idea of what my life is all about, he thought.

He asked the officer to buckle him into the van, and the officer obliged. The officer also brought ankle shackles with him so that Greg wouldn't run again—and which ensured that Greg would have to do the infamous perp shuffle when he arrived for booking.

Greg was prepared for the officers to take him and the others on a "rough ride," slamming on the brakes and all that. He was pleasantly surprised when they didn't, though he figured that the ones who would have done so just weren't driving that day.

He considered himself lucky when he got to his holding cell unscathed. Some of the guys came into central booking with huge knots on their heads, split lips, or bloody noses; one came in limping. Another one arrived freshly shuttled in from the hospital, still wearing a bloody gown.

Greg was pissed that he'd gotten caught. After the day he'd had, the arrest had forced him to relinquish back to the man the power the streets had given him. But he leaned back, shut his eyes, and prepared for the long road ahead, grateful to be a black man who attempted to flee police and lived to tell about it.

TUESDAY, APRIL 28

Anthony

Anthony's pace quickened. Tuesday was supposed to be his day off, the one day a week the Bake was closed. On any normal Tuesday morning he would be just waking up after a late Monday night at the Shake & Bake. But this Tuesday morning he was speed-walking down Pennsylvania Avenue as the sun beat down on him.

He studied the damaged buildings as he walked past them. He'd intentionally parked almost a mile away from his normal spot right in front of Shake & Bake because he wanted to walk the neighborhood and see firsthand what Monday evening had wrought. Anthony lived in Towson, Maryland, a suburban enclave about fifteen minutes outside of Baltimore City. When he locked the doors at Shake & Bake on Monday, he'd thought the worst of the night was over. The violence in Penn North had already started, but in his mind it seemed relatively controlled and restricted. Anthony went home Monday night insecure about the future of Baltimore but not worried about his place of employment—Shake & Bake was about nine blocks away from the infamous intersection where the CVS and cars were on fire, capturing international attention.

Tuesday morning, his phone rang at eight. Already up, he answered on the first ring.

"Ms. Gloria, how you?"

Ms. Gloria lived near Shake & Bake and was a mainstay of the community. She immediately launched into a rundown of the events from the night before, her Baltimore twang becoming more animated as she went on. She told him about the looting—it might have started in Penn North, but as the evening progressed it had worked its way down Pennsylvania Avenue. The Korean-owned grocery store, the Downtown Locker Room with its familiar beet-red DTLR sign over the door, the check-cashing store—all of them were now either burned out or with gaping holes where glass windows used to be, shelves emptied.

Ms. Gloria went into detail about the intensity of the night, how fast everything had seemed to move. The police had usually been nowhere to be found—and when they were on the scene, they'd showed no interest in stopping the chaos.

Then, Ms. Gloria went on, the crowd kept moving farther east down Pennsylvania Avenue, and by the early morning hours they had reached the Shake & Bake.

Anthony braced himself for the worst.

But Ms. Gloria, pride in her voice, described an unbelievable scene. Malik and a group of other Shake & Bake loyalists met the crowd. They stood in front of the building, arms locked, backs straight, and shouted to the angry crowd that they needed to move on. Ms. Gloria recited to Anthony verbatim what Malik had yelled at the protesters as they moved closer to Shake & Bake: "This black owned, yo! All this down the street is black. You need to move on."

As Anthony listened to Ms. Gloria, he recalled what Malik had told him a few days back: "Ain't no way they gon' burn the Bake." When Anthony had heard Malik say this, he thought the young man just meant the Bake would not be a target. Listening to Ms. Gloria, he now realized that Malik had meant they wouldn't burn the Bake because Malik wouldn't allow it. Anthony listened in satisfaction. It wasn't simply that his young people had protected his business; it was that he knew their commitment to Shake & Bake was a return on what he had invested in those young people, in his community.

Anthony had been two years old when the Baltimore riots of April 1968 took place. That was when Baltimore, along with more than a hundred other cities around the country, suffered through a spasm of riots after the brutal assassination of Dr. Martin Luther King Jr. Thousands of National Guardsmen and hundreds of Maryland state policemen descended upon Baltimore during eight days of civil unrest that culminated in five deaths and more than five thousand arrests.

The dynamics of Baltimore in 2015 mirrored those of 1968 in that even though the death of one person—Freddie Gray or Dr. King—might have been the spark, the social conditions in Baltimore were what had allowed the flame to burn so hot. The riots around the murder of Dr. King had been driven by a sense that a dream had been shattered. The uprising around the death of Freddie Gray was a response to the generations-long nightmare that followed, a dream deferred.

Now Anthony walked past familiar faces as he got closer to Shake & Bake on Tuesday morning. Young people asked him what size sneakers he wore, in case he wanted to buy some new kicks; Anthony knew that those were sneakers that just the day before had been sitting in the now-busted display cases up and down the avenue.

When Anthony had first woken up that morning at five-thirty, he had immediately turned on the television and watched the reports from the night before in heartbreak and disbelief. He lay in bed and despondently turned from the national shows to the local news. There he saw a story that not only caught his eye but made him sit up.

The story began with the same image of the burning CVS that the other news outlets had been replaying, with people running into the store empty-handed but leaving with diapers, baby formula, paper towels, candy bars, and anything else they could carry out. It was a mix of opportunism and necessity— and people rushing to take advantage of a total breakdown.

But the next image on the local news was one he had not seen yet. It was from that morning, not the night before. The CVS was no longer burning but burned out. In front of it was a young girl, no more than ten years old, wearing jeans, a T-shirt, and yellow work gloves. In her hands she grasped a shovel that seemed to be as tall as she was. Over and over again she shoveled away trash and debris, both remnants and symbols of the night before. Anthony could not take his eyes off this little girl, who first thing in the morning wasn't dwelling on what went wrong but had her eyes on what was next. She was strong and beautiful. She was resilient. She was Baltimore. And when Anthony saw her that morning, his immediate instinct was that his day off was not going to be a day off. He got up from his bed and started to get dressed.

Jenny

O N Tuesday Jenny woke up with no voice, the result of just three hours of sleep and irritation from the smoke of the fires the night before. Although it was a weekday, there was no court, and school had been canceled. Public defenders are state employees and had been excused from work for the day, along with the rest of the city. But the number of arrestees from the day before now topped two hundred, and Jenny caught wind that children were among them. So she headed straight to the makeshift law office at the Real News building downtown near City Hall, passing through eerily quiet streets. It was the first time in days that the city had been quiet.

By midmorning, Jenny knew something was wrong. Maryland law required that arrestees see a court commissioner within twenty-four hours. By midafternoon, only twelve people had—and they had been arrested on Saturday. She discovered that Governor Larry Hogan had suspended habeas corpus, allowing the police to jail protesters without filing charging documents.

Jenny began researching, looking for a recourse. She connected her fellow public defenders to the experts—the NAACP Legal Defense Fund and the Ferguson Legal Defense Committee, who had managed the fallout from other historic uprisings. And then she went to find the children.

When she arrived at Baltimore Central Booking and Intake Facility, she was pleased to find that a bunch of public defenders were already there. They were documenting arrestees, since there was no paper trail for the arrests.

She walked through the usually bustling halls of Central Booking, which were eerily quiet, especially after a night of mayhem. Commissioner booths were empty, so she followed her intuition and wandered around until she happened upon the court commissioners' suite. She was happy to see about ten commissioners huddled around a table, even more than on a normal day. She figured they'd been called in to process the protesters who had been arrested the day before.

The hum of conversation in the room stopped when the commissioners saw her. Questioning eyes met hers. Then she looked down at what was on the table in front of them.

These people are eating cake?

She stood for a few moments staring stupidly at the large grocery store sheet cake they were devouring. An awkward amount of time passed before she said the first thing that came to mind.

"Hi, I'm Jenny," she said to the group.

One commissioner was polite enough to introduce herself back.

"So, are there any hearings happening?" Jenny asked.

"Not right now."

"Can you tell me why?" she asked.

They all peered down at their plates of half-eaten cake.

John

JOHN LOOSENED HIS TIE AND undid the top button of his shirt, then went back to his phone call.

Freddie Gray's funeral happened to fall on the day scheduled for the start of an Orioles home stand, with the Chicago White Sox the first team coming in to play the Birds. An American League rival who were experiencing a bit of a revival of their own, the White Sox were the favorite team of President Obama. The scrappy sibling of the Chicago baseball rivalry, they always seemed to be playing with a chip on their shoulder. This home stand was important to the Orioles. Winning offered them a chance to show that their recent dominance of the American League was not a fluke.

Late Monday afternoon the players were already at the stadium, preparing for the 7:05 P.M. start. Workers had already begun preparing the concession stands. The gates opened ninety minutes before the scheduled first pitch, so there were only a small number of fans in the park at 5:45 to hear the announcement over the PA that the Orioles had made the decision to postpone the game and that everyone needed to leave the stadium and head home. What those in attendance didn't yet know was that the governor had just declared a state of emergency in the city of Baltimore, and the Maryland National Guard was preparing to enter the city.

Now, on Tuesday, the person who'd been at the center of the decision to cancel the game on Monday sat with the phone pressed against his ear. His neck might have been liberated from the constraining Windsor knot, but John Angelos was feeling the weight of having to make the same choice for a second day in a row.

The final decision about whether or not to play a Major League Baseball game is made by the home team. There have been many reasons games have been postponed or their location moved, safety being the common denominator. Storms, particularly those involving lightning or heavy rains, are easy decisions. Flooding, snow, and high winds have also led teams to make the decision that it's better to give up the $2 million in economic activity generated by the average baseball game than to play the game and have something go horribly wrong. These decisions are not taken lightly, and they are not made before consulting with every potentially impacted partner. So in Baltimore, the mayor's office, the Maryland Stadium Authority (which manages and maintains both Camden Yards and nearby M&T Bank Stadium), the police department, meteorologists, and a number of others all have a voice, but the final say belongs to the Orioles.

John listened to every one of the arguments for and against postponing. With the city under a state of emergency and a newly imposed curfew, there were certain hard limitations. Yes, in principle the mayor's office could declare that the curfew applied to everyone except those attending the baseball game, but both practically and symbolically that was never an option for City Hall. What about moving the time of the game earlier, so that the game would be over and fans and staff could be home well before the curfew? Many of the people who had tickets for that game would probably still be at work when the game started at its new time, and might not be able to go. Plus the Orioles would have to spend the same amount of money for security, concessions, cleaning, and so on, but with a smaller number of fans there would be less revenue from sales of food and souvenirs.

There was one other option that seemed uniquely logical: holding the game a forty-five-minute drive away at Nationals Park in Washington, DC, home of the Washington Nationals. Washington has always been all about politics, but it has also been about baseball games. Between 1901 and 1960 congressmen and blue-collar workers alike could go watch the Washington Senators run around the bases on steamy summer days. After the Senators moved to Minnesota and became the Twins, the District was without baseball for decades. But when the Montreal Expos' owner sold the team to Major League Baseball in 2001, MLB began looking for a new home for the team. Oklahoma City, Portland, and San Juan, Puerto Rico, all vied to host the franchise. But on December 3, 2004, the major league club owners voted nearly unanimously that Washington should be the home of the newly named Nationals. The District yearned for a baseball team, and the potential for revenue was high. Locating a team there would create a natural rivalry between the Washington and Baltimore teams, similar to when the Cubs and the White Sox squared off in Chicago or when the Mets and Yankees battled in their brutal Subway Series in New York. This all made sense, and the owners were excited. The vote was 28–1. The only dissenter was Peter Angelos, the owner of the Baltimore Orioles.

Once the transfer was official, the Battle for the Beltway quickly became more than the nickname for the contests between the two teams. Soon another partnership between the Orioles and the Nationals was born: MASN, or the Mid-Atlantic Sports Network. This regional network would broadcast sports events in the region, ranging from horse racing and college sports to Orioles, Nationals, and Ravens games. This highly profitable venture was first structured with the Orioles owning 90 percent of the product and paying the Washington Nationals $20 million a year for the rights to broadcast the Nationals games to the full regional audience. In 2012 the teams began renegotiating the deal. The Nationals wanted to receive more than $100 million annually from MASN because of the popularity of their team and growth of their franchise. The Orioles countered with just shy of $40 million, a doubling of the initial deal but a fraction of the ask. The Orioles thought that offer was generous, but the Nationals found it offensive, and it led to a string of subtle and not-so-subtle barbs lobbed up and down Interstate 95, and lingering bad feelings.

This background explained the contempt from both sides when baseball's newly appointed commissioner, Rob Manfred, made the suggestion that the Orioles–White Sox game should be played at Nationals Park. The Nationals were away during that time, so the stadium would be empty, and it was only thirty miles from Camden Yards, making it seemingly the simplest, most elegant, and least disruptive solution. But the O's never even really considered it—they would rather postpone Tuesday's game than play a "home" game in enemy territory.

So the Orioles prepared to announce that for the second time in two days the team's game would be postponed. But

during all of the back-and-forth, John had heard one suggestion that would not leave his mind. The idea had been tossed
out almost in jest, and was almost instantly ignored as everyone went on to the next option. But John kept wondering:
What if we played a game with no fans?

Anthony

Anthony peered over the steering wheel, taking in everything around him as the car traveled at ten miles per hour past friends and neighbors. He was driving the only car in a procession of almost twenty people who had left Shake & Bake minutes before and were on their way to the intersection of Pennsylvania and North Avenues.

When Anthony had arrived at Shake & Bake earlier that day, he called up G., his longtime friend and a fixture at the rink. G. was one of the top skaters at the Bake, one of the handful of people Anthony thought were truly magic on eight wheels. Anthony knew that Shake & Bake needed to respond to the uprising, and after last night it seemed clear that the rink could be part of some sort of solution. He wasn't sure what it would look like, but he wasn't going to wait for instructions. He thought of the young girl he'd seen on the news that morning picking up trash and the dozens of people who'd joined her throughout the city of Baltimore that day. He told G. to call up a few of the regular skaters and see if they would be willing to come by Shake & Bake for a conversation about how they could be part of some sort of healing. Within an hour, fifteen people showed up.

Malik hadn't slept the night before and walked into the Bake looking defeated. He questioned the idea when he first heard it. His eyes were downcast and his spirit seemed broken. Anthony pulled him aside and told him how much he needed him. He reminded him how much the young boys looked up to him, and then he told him he'd heard what Malik had done the night before and how much he appreciated it.

Malik was bone-weary and frustrated. But before him stood his role model telling him that he needed him. And Malik knew there was only one right answer.

So that was how Anthony came to be driving very slowly toward Penn North with more than a dozen skaters around him, some holding on to the car and some skating alongside it.

Anthony came to a wooden barricade set up in the middle of the street and pulled to a stop. He spied his friend Father Charles Hall, the pastor of St. Peter Claver Church, in the street, and they shared a smile. Father Hall's salt-and-pepper hair, heavyset frame, and friendly grin felt like a warm welcome to Anthony. He watched Father Hall briefly converse with the National Guardsman who stood in front of the barricade, which had been erected to keep vehicles from passing. The guardsmen gripped their weapons tightly. Anthony gripped the steering wheel.

Eventually one of the guard members waved a colleague over, and the two soldiers lifted the wooden barrier and gestured for Anthony and his squad of roller skaters to go on by. He wasn't sure exactly how Father Hall had convinced the

National Guard to let them pass, but Anthony moved his foot to the gas and resumed his slow pace down the street.

As he made his way past the barricade, Anthony rolled down the window to say thank you. Father Hall smiled and extended his hand. "God bless you, brother."

Jenny

EVEN THE PRESIDENT CALLED THEM thugs. Jenny felt it was the typical, lazy way of characterizing the young people, mostly boys, who came to her for help. The comment roiled many in Baltimore. The city understood respectability politics but didn't respect it. Particularly when it always seemed the respectability part didn't pertain to its citizens. Only the politics.

There were certain unique pressures Barack Obama had to endure. He seemed to constantly be walking a fine line of being true to himself while keeping white Americans at ease with the fresh phenomenon of an African American president. From his campaign (Jeremiah Wright, the Philadelphia speech, the moment when he gave his wife a societally ubiquitous fist bump and Fox News coined the term "terrorist fist jab" to describe it) to the earliest days of his presidency, it was clear that the standard when it came to talking about race in a nuanced fashion would be significantly different for this president, and therefore his willingness to do so with a degree of honesty would be compromised.

Six years before Freddie was loaded into the back of a police van, and a little under four hundred miles away from Baltimore, Harvard professor and world-renowned public intellectual Dr. Henry Louis Gates Jr. returned home from a trip to China, where he had been researching the ancestry of Yo-Yo Ma, the cellist, for his popular PBS show. When he tried to enter his home he found the front door jammed shut, so with the help of his driver he tried to force it open. Someone saw them and called the police, reporting two African Americans trying to break into a home. After the responding officer arrived, Dr. Gates, wearing a red striped short-sleeved polo shirt and using a cane, was arrested in his own home. The charges were dropped five days after the arrest, but by that time a national conversation had begun. On July 22, 2009, at a press conference about health care reform, the new president of the United States was asked about the incident and what it meant for race relations. The president paused and responded, "Now, I've—I don't know, not having been there and not seeing all the facts, what role race played in that. But I think it's fair to say, number one, any of us would be pretty angry; number two, that the Cambridge police acted stupidly in arresting somebody when there was already proof that they were in their own home; and number three, what I think we know separate and apart from this incident is that there is a long history in this country of African Americans and Latinos being stopped by law enforcement disproportionately. That's just a fact."

The right-wing media swiftly condemned the new president, arguing that he was overly racializing the incident and introducing "radical" language into the debate. The president of the Fraternal Order of Police Florida State Lodge, James Preston, said, "To make such an offhanded comment about a subject without the benefit of facts, in such a public forum, hurts police/community relations and is a setback to years of progress." A Pew opinion poll taken right after the incident showed that 41 percent of people disapproved of Obama's handling of the situation, while only 29 percent approved. Tellingly, his overall support among white voters dropped seven points in its aftermath. Two days after responding to the impromptu question, the president apologized and walked back his comments. The incident culminated on July 30, when, after an invitation from the president, Dr. Gates and the officer who had arrested him, Sgt. James Crowley, joined Obama for the infamous "beer summit" to discuss the situation over pints of ale. The meeting was superficially a success, with polls indicating that the public approved. Dr. Gates and Sgt. Crowley both released statements praising the president's leadership and push toward reconciliation. Dr. Gates called the president "very wise, very sage, very Solomonic." But the praise was not universal; many were left frustrated and bothered that the reaction to a fifty-eight-year-old African American professor being arrested in his own home was a "beer summit," carrying the suggestion that both parties—the professor arrested in his own home and the officer who did it—were somehow equivalent. They were bothered that the president had been compelled to walk back his mild initial comment, which many felt was a simple and overdue statement of truth that didn't need clarification. In retracting his initial comments about Officer Crowley, Obama gave the officer the benefit of the doubt. So when the president called the young men in Baltimore thugs, many assumed the same offer would not be extended to them.

Jenny knew one of the children who was being badmouthed. The young man had decided to pick up a rock and hurl it at a police officer. It was one of the scenes that had flashed across television screens countrywide, one of the images that spurred even the most powerful man in the world to write it off as an act of pointless violence rather than an act of vengeance.

Just a few weeks before the protests, the young man had finally gotten back into Frederick Douglass High School. He was diagnosed with cognitive and learning disabilities. But he was smart enough to know what had happened to his uncle.

It was the first memory he had of the police. In 2007, when he was around ten years old, his uncle had what would become a fatal encounter with police. In news reports, the police department said officers approached twenty-five-year-old Jay Cook, who they believed "was walking in a manner that indicated he had a gun." Cook was known to police because he had been arrested for armed robbery and carjacking but never convicted. When he saw them that day in 2007, he ran. The police chased him. What came next is one of the many stories of what happens to a young man running while black from police in Baltimore.

Cook allegedly came to a six-foot chain-link fence, squeezed through, and emerged onto a bridge atop westbound US 40. He dangled from the overpass briefly before he fell to his death, hit by a car in rush-hour traffic.

The police said he slipped, but when his young nephew saw Jay in the casket, he thought otherwise.

"I remember his fingers," the boy would tell Jenny in one of their interviews.

In 2017, an investigative report by *Reveal*/WYPR examined the details of Jay Cook's case. It found that Cook had gone out to buy a money order, and because he had been robbed at gunpoint the week before, he ran when he saw figures moving toward him. Witnesses said they saw him clinging for his life. It was revealed that police reports were inaccurate. In a depo-

sition, an officer wept as he described his attempt to save Jay,
confessing that when he fell a white officer said: "It's just one
less nigger we have to deal with." While a lawsuit was filed,
inaccurate police reports caused the suit to be dismissed, and
ultimately his family failed to get justice.

His uncle's death became a source of pain for Jenny's client.
The police officers who patrolled his school knew it. They
would bring it up when they saw him, knowing it would make
him snap. And it wasn't long before they got him right where
they wanted him—in handcuffs, in school.

He was attending Digital Harbor High School when this
boiled over. It was a typical day for a student with special
needs: he got irritated and began to go on a profanity-laced
tirade against the aide assigned to stay close to him in order to
guide him and help him. The behavioral plan for students with
special needs anticipates these kinds of flare-ups and outlines
a process for deescalating them to avoid punitive discipline or
suspension. The boy and his aide were preparing to take a
walk, the way they did whenever he needed to calm down,
when a school police officer walked past the door.

"Shut your damn mouth. You can't talk like that in school,"
the cop told him.

"Fuck you," the boy said.

Before he'd even finished saying it, the officer tackled him to
the ground and silenced him with a punch. That was how
Jenny met him at Baby Booking, getting his first charge. He
was expelled from school, and that was it—he was in the system. Through the school-to-prison pipeline in a flash.

By the time April 27 rolled around, he was back on track. A
few weeks before, Jenny had helped to get him back to school,
this time Frederick Douglass High. He was calm until he saw
the damn officer. The one who'd taunted him about his uncle.

The one who'd teased him for being dumb. The one who'd jacked him up, arrested him. The officer had the nerve to be posing as a protector in riot gear. And so a rock flew.

Jenny was proud of the boy. She knew it wasn't right to throw rocks at the police, or anybody else, but all humans have a right to defend their honor. And the United States is a country based on a revolution, born of people who fought back, Jenny thought. Even if it comes at a cost.

The system certainly made the teen pay. He was on juvenile probation when he threw the rock in April, but he wasn't charged with assaulting a police officer for throwing the rock until August. This time, he was charged as an adult, and held on an astronomically high $150,000 bail. And the system made sure he would never stop paying: he was convicted of second-degree assault, which is a felony, which means it never comes off your record. He was sentenced in January 2016, serving one year in prison and three years' probation. He never got to graduate from Douglass.

Jenny had long had a front-row seat to the way the justice system preyed on youth. George had taught her that. He was her first Innocence Project client, convicted of rape at nineteen. He was a drug abuser who'd spent his early years in and out of the juvenile justice system. He had been picked up and charged with the rape because he was a heroin addict; the police knew he wouldn't be able to remember where he'd been three months earlier, when the girl said that a man matching his description had violated her.

Decades later, they finally ran prints from a rape kit they'd found while clearing out a storage unit. The prints were traced back to a serial rapist who had been picked up on a college campus just two months before George was arrested.

By the time his name was cleared, George was almost sixty. He had served thirty-nine years for a crime he didn't commit. Jenny had vowed that from that day on she'd fight for those who couldn't fight for themselves.

And that was why Jenny had to find the children.

Anthony

Anthony hadn't felt joy in a week. In the ten days since the marching began, Anthony had watched his revenue drop off a cliff and he wasn't sure what to do about it. Anthony would agonize with his wife for countless hours, wondering what he would do if things did not pick up. He told her that for the first time ever, Shake & Bake had begun feeling like a "job." But on this day he was reminded that it was everything he had in the world.

When he'd called the skaters to Shake & Bake that day, he'd told them that it was a way for them to discuss what they could do to lift the collective soul of the city. They couldn't give speeches because no one would come to hear them speak. They couldn't give money because they were all living paycheck to paycheck. They couldn't register people to vote because no significant election would take place for more than a year. But they could skate.

What Anthony hadn't really known to tell them was that it wasn't just the city's soul that needed healing, but his too. Anthony sincerely wanted to help the city, but beneath that was his own search for comfort, to know that all that he'd committed to this community—the time and emotional labor he'd invested over so much of his life—was worth it.

Now Anthony stood outside his car, reached his hand in through the window, and turned the stereo volume all the way up.

With Marvin Gaye's "What's Going On" blasting from Anthony's car speakers, Malik, G., and the other skaters formed a large circle and skated around Penn North as dozens of onlookers cheered. In perfect rhythm, the skaters pivoted, spun, and did other things on skates that most of the people watching couldn't do in sneakers. But the bystanders could sing, and they did, singing along to Marvin's smooth notes and cheering as the skaters dazzled with their grace and generosity. Twenty-four hours earlier, this same intersection had swarmed with fire trucks and news crews, a symbol not just of the breakdown of the city but of the breakdown of confidence in that city.

Now, though, Anthony, eyes closed, toothy grin shining, clapped to the beat as the skaters twirled. Hoping that a restoration in confidence would move to a beat.

John

J OHN DROVE QUICKLY DOWN PRATT Street, a main corridor connecting the interstate with downtown Baltimore. It was well after ten o'clock, and the curfew was now in full effect. Twenty-four hours earlier, the National Guard had taken up positions in the city of Baltimore. Police officers fanned out around the city, many still in riot gear. The streets were quiet, so the gear was more a show of force than a necessity. Warriors ready for war while simultaneously trying to keep it from happening.

John hadn't known what he would find once he entered the city. He'd expected checkpoints and barricades. He'd fully expected to be fined for being out on the roads after the curfew. The city was under a state of emergency. The night before there'd been riots and burned buildings, millions of dollars of damage. John had been half expecting a scene out of Beirut, Tikrit, or Kandahar. But what he found as he drove his Jeep Cherokee back into the city was, in a word, Baltimore. The Baltimore he knew. The Baltimore he lived in. The Baltimore he called home.

He'd heard the governor and mayor tell people to stay home or risk arrest. He'd watched the press conference where the police commissioner, with his pressed white uniform and the brilliant gold stars adorning his collar, stressed the seriousness of the curfew, emphasizing that officers would be checking IDs for ages of kids and verifying addresses to make sure that men were at their home of record. Not being there could result in handcuffs. Tonight, though, weaving through the downtown streets, John simply nodded at officers as he breezed past them. Feelings of relief and bewilderment jostled inside him as he realized that the application of what were supposed to be citywide rules seemed discretionary.

He thought of a famous Benjamin Franklin quote: "Those who would give up essential Liberty, to purchase a little temporary Safety, deserve neither Liberty nor Safety." But there were those who didn't have to sacrifice either. The fear that consumed the city was real and shared. Arguably for the first time, an evenly distributed burden of uncertainty crossed neighborhood boundaries. But the burden of control wasn't evenly distributed. The distance between inconvenience and oppression seemed color-coded.

As he freely moved through the downtown streets past high-priced condos and Starbucks coffee shops, John realized the curfew was not for him.

WEDNESDAY, APRIL 29

Partee

SURROUNDED BY OFFICERS HE'D MET for the first time just hours before, Partee slowly strolled between Camden Yards and M&T Bank Stadium. The two stadiums had been built in downtown Baltimore around the same time and with the same goal: to celebrate professional sports in a city that bled for it while driving economic impact in a city that needed it. M&T Bank Stadium was where the Baltimore Ravens, those purple-and-black gridiron warriors, did battle eight Sundays a year. Within eyeshot was Camden Yards, where the Baltimore Orioles raced around basepaths. Placing the stadiums so close to each other was deliberate. Sports fans near and far did not have to be confused as to where to go to be entertained. Downtown Baltimore was the destination.

Standing around the stadium with a legion of out-of-town cops from neighboring municipalities like Prince George's County and Howard County was not Partee's normal job. As a police major, he had a significant jurisdiction he was responsible for and hundreds of officers who fell under his command. He hadn't walked a beat for many, many years, not since he first joined the police force. But going toe-to-toe with the police chief had consequences. So today, instead of spending the morning leading the officers he was trained to lead, he was patrolling with officers he didn't even know.

The night before, Partee had gotten a call from his boss, Lt. Col. Miller: "I need you to come in and report to Camden Yards. Going to place you with some dispatched officers." Partee was furious, because he knew exactly what that meant: he was essentially being demoted, no longer trusted or empowered to lead officers. Instead, he was going to a quiet area to serve as a glorified security guard. He wanted to protest, but he had no energy left to fight. He responded with "Yes, sir" instead of the "Whatever" that was his first impulse. He'd known that his interaction on Monday with Commissioner Batts would have repercussions; he just hadn't been sure of what they would be or when they would come down. He worried for his job, for his livelihood, for his passion.

The Prince George's County cops he met looked at him with a mixture of awe and disbelief. The awe was because they all had heard the folklore about Partee's actions on Monday— that he'd been running around without a helmet, pulling his fellow officers out of harm's way; that he'd been riding on the side of a BearCat armored personnel carrier throwing teargas in order to disperse crowds; that he'd jumped out of trees onto criminals and run up the hill by himself dodging bricks. Partee shook his head when they recounted these stories to him, telling them that not everything they heard was true. Details aside, though, they knew that Partee had met an extraordinary day with extraordinary courage. The disbelief was because this now legendary police major from Baltimore was doing beat cop patrols with a group of out-of-towners.

Commissioner Batts was the top cop in Baltimore City, and

Partee was certain his insubordination was not going to be taken lightly. But when Batts approached him on Monday, West Baltimore had been under siege, and Partee was watching his officers getting hurt. At that moment, Batts's seniority didn't matter to Partee. But now Partee realized that Batts didn't care about Partee's seniority, either.

He wasn't mad at Miller; he knew his direct boss was just the messenger. He was mad at the entire structure. But when he showed up for work and reported to the Maryland State Police's big mobile command post, he asked the duty sergeant for a list of the daily reporting meetings. This was a normal request for an officer of his rank and authority. But the sergeant made it very clear to him that the state officers would be taking over the real work from there. From the moment that Governor Larry Hogan—in office for only three months at that point—stood in front of cameras on Monday night announcing he was deploying the National Guard to Baltimore, the message was glaringly evident: the state thought the Baltimore City police force was inept. During Hogan's announcement the mayor sat stone-faced behind the governor, knowing that much of the blame, fairly or unfairly, was headed her way. Governor Hogan, in short sleeves, his face steely and serious, projected the image of calm competence the city needed. Partee had heard loud and clear the subtext he was sending to the city and the world: that Baltimore City needed to stand down and allow the adults to take over.

The parking lot that Partee patrolled stood silent and empty moments before the start of an Orioles game. Partee stared at the out-of-town officers around him, all wearing different uniforms than he was, and wondered how he'd gotten there.

Jenny

THE HABEAS CORPUS PETITIONS WENT out en masse on
Wednesday from the tired group of public defenders, led
by Jenny's colleague Natalie Finegar, who had stayed up all
night. By midafternoon, the public defender's office got word
that hundreds of arrested protesters would be released. At
least one hundred began to be released, half on their own re-
cognizance, many on astronomically high bails.

Most of the city was still shut down, but the juvenile courts
had opened solely for the children who were arrested in the
protests. About five attorneys from Jenny's office had gone to
represent the defendants in court hearings—all told, forty-
nine kids. The state's attorney dismissed twenty-one cases
without even bringing them to court, so the attorneys tag-
teamed on the remaining twenty-eight hearings, some for ado-
lescents who had been held since Saturday. Police officials
admitted they had not provided due process to all who were
detained but explained that they had been overwhelmed, that
they were just rounding them up and shuttling them out of the

chaos of the protests. In defending themselves, law enforcement officials pointed to the 1968 riots, when more than five thousand people were arrested and hundreds were held in jail for days before appearing in court because arrest records went missing. History was just repeating itself, with different excuses.

Jenny wanted to give the police the benefit of the doubt, but the truth was that at this point they deserved none.

One of her clients had been protesting at the Western District, but he wasn't arrested there. He was in his house when the cops barged in through the door, tackled him, and arrested him. He was then held for days in juvenile lockup with no probable cause. Eventually he was released after seeing a judge, but the fact that he had been illegally arrested in the first place was never addressed. Meanwhile, Jenny knew that the police were retaliating against the boy—they wanted to make sure he knew that when all was said and done, they could still get to him without consequence. Jenny had several other clients who were arrested with no police reports, no charges, basic violations of their rights. And everyone let it happen, from the police to the state's attorney to the Department of Juvenile Services. Even after all that had happened, Jenny was still shocked at how quickly fealty to the law and the principles behind it could fall away.

The vast majority of kids who were being held at the Baltimore City Detention Center (BCDC) were released that day, and many of them were back on the streets marching by that evening. Around 6:00 P.M., as she worked alone in her office, Jenny could see them as they passed the Juvenile Justice Building on Gay Street. As she watched them heading down Gay Street, Jenny snapped a picture from her office and breathed a sigh of relief. They were out, they were free, and they weren't cowed.

At 6:44 P.M. she sent a message to her wife: "100+ detainees being released from BCDC due to the brief we prepped last night. Huge victory!"

Nick

THE TOWERING REDBRICK BUILDING THAT housed Carver Vocational-Technical High School buzzed with commotion. Of the nearly one thousand students enrolled, nearly all of them seemed ready to resume classes and get back to the normalcy of a traditional high school experience. Home of the Bears, Carver was better-known for producing electricians and carpenters than five-star athletic recruits. Nevertheless, Nick moved toward the manicured baseball diamond. He and his staff were holding boxes of pizza, almost three dozen in total, eliciting cheers and smiles from the students.

Before visiting Carver, Nick had spent much of the day touring around his district, meeting with students, shop owners, and residents alike, trying to understand where people were and then sharing his discoveries. He took pictures of open stores where people were lining up to purchase everyday necessities, the buses packed with employees on their way to work—the ordinariness of West Baltimore movement—and tweeted them out.

He did so not to prove a point, but to counter the point that

others were making. The prevailing narrative was that Baltimore was a war zone, its buildings still smoldering, violent
eruptions further splintering an already fractured city. Most
of the narratives were being driven by people who had only
passed through Baltimore on their way to Washington, DC,
via Amtrak train, or those who wanted to know where the
"worst areas" were so that they could station their video cameras there. Nick wanted to share his view. His vision. His
home.

At Carver he watched the kids running the bases, sliding
into home, scoring another run for their team. He witnessed
how other students came to cheer on their classmates, the
Bears, who represented their school against other Baltimore
schools. He wondered why the Orioles did not have the same
level of courage. He thought their decision to play the White
Sox without any fans present was a weak one. He was frustrated by the idea of the city being kept out of Camden Yards,
forced to serve as unseen characters in a story about the city's
unevenness. Why not play the damn game with people in the
stands? he wondered. To play a game with no fans would only
serve to bolster the idea that Baltimore was beyond repair—
and that its students, specifically its black students, were the
reason for it. So he cheered for the students at Carver as if they
had "Baltimore" written on their uniforms, because in his eyes
they represented what the city was: resilient, irrepressible,
buoyant.

The kids Nick watched knew their fair share of inconsistencies and violence. For a city that averaged almost one homicide
a day—although East and West Baltimore suffered the bulk of
the carnage—the paradox was that during the days of the uprising, the street violence in the city actually ceased. During
the time between Freddie Gray being laid to rest and the

students from Carver taking the field, only one homicide in Baltimore had been recorded, according to the Baltimore City Police Department. (Carver, incidentally, had been the last school that Freddie Gray attended.)

Nick spoke with students and laughed on that cloudless spring day. As the kids ate pizza, he picked up a bat and shared anecdotes about his prowess on the baseball diamond, as well as biographical illustrations of legends long gone. He thought of his own kids, his gorgeous daughters, who would grow up in the same city that raised him. He hoped to make their path easier, less traumatic. Hoped that they'd grow up in a Baltimore where there wouldn't have to be a debate about whether they could find opportunities if they stayed. Staying in Baltimore should not have to coincide with disappointment.

Nick had been up and moving since six that morning, walking his district, taking pictures and tweeting about Baltimore rising. Baltimore arisen. But when he returned home later that evening, the house would be empty. Fearing for their children's safety, he and his wife had decided to send the kids out of town to stay with his sisters for a while.

Tawanda

TAWANDA SAT IN FRONT OF a dozen young children whose eyes were dancing. She was in the place she was most comfortable, the space she'd been born to stand in: the role of educator. She'd been a teacher for a little over a decade, and now was teaching pre-kindergarten in Towson at an independent preschool program. For most of the children she worked with, Ms. Tawanda was the first teacher they would meet, and she took that seriously.

She led the class of children, about half boys and half girls, half black and half white, in the way she always did, with songs and smiles. The children loved the gold fronts on Tawanda's front teeth—she showed them off, and the children reciprocated, showing off the gaps created by their newly lost baby teeth. They were so innocent and blameless. They were back in the KinderCare program for the first time since Monday, but had no idea why it was closed the day before.

Towson was on the outskirts of Baltimore City, about twenty miles from where Tawanda grew up and only a few miles from where she lived now. She'd believed when she first moved from Baltimore City to quieter Baltimore County that it would be enough of a buffer to provide her and her family with more safety and security. She hoped the suburbs would provide more options for her and her family. She marveled at the start the kids at her school were receiving. These young children, not even in kindergarten yet, knew their numbers, letters, colors, and basic math. Most of the kids there had similar middle-class backgrounds, but going to school with kids who looked different offered a glimpse into the diverse world they would soon inherit. This school was a place where their presence was greeted with promise and excitement, so different from the world she'd come up in—the world that had taken her brother.

Tawanda had different themes on different days. Some days the kids would come in dressed as superheroes. On others the kids would have show-and-tell. Today the kids would be talking about what they wanted to do when they got older. Some wanted to be teachers like Ms. Tawanda. Some wanted to be firefighters. Some came wearing doctors' outfits and stethoscopes. The colorful descriptions warmed Tawanda's heart. Almost a third wanted to be police officers, like Steven, a four-year-old with blue Crocs and a fresh haircut, his straight brown locks peeking from underneath his navy blue toy police cap. The costume onesie he wore featured a badge alongside other police insignia and a red tie. Tawanda smiled and asked why he wanted to be a police officer. He proudly replied that he wanted to help people. Tawanda loved his answer. She placed her hands on his shoulders, her smile meeting his. "That's great that you want to be a police officer. Just make sure you are a good officer. Just be the best officer you can be and help as many people as you can."

Greg

G REG WATCHED DROVES OF PEOPLE leave the jail on
Wednesday, including one of his friends from the neighborhood. It had been two days since they had all been arrested,
and it seemed that only Greg would remain in detention. He
was on lockdown, so he didn't have access to information about
what was going on in the outside world—the releases were
the only sign of what was happening beyond the jailhouse
walls. He wondered if anyone was looking for him. But then
again, he had given the cops a fake name. How would anyone
even find him?

Time stood still. He had been spending his days doing push-
ups, watching TV, and eating food that he wouldn't have fed
his pit bull. He did have some good conversations with his fellow prisoners, though. One of the most memorable was with a
middle-aged white dude whom Greg walked the cell with in
circles one night when neither of them could sleep.

"What are you in for?" the man asked him.

"Man, I'm in here for my people," Greg said.

Greg knew that he had done something big, etched himself

in Baltimore's history. He had even signed a few autographs once people figured out who he was, what he'd done. But he couldn't stop thinking about that moment with the fire hose. Why hadn't he just kept throwing bottles at the police? The reality was he had nothing against the fire department; he never saw them as a source of oppression or pain. They didn't sit around letting black people burn in buildings, taking two hours to respond because they stopped for sandwiches on their way to a low-income neighborhood. He told himself that even if he'd directed his anger that day at the wrong people, in that moment he didn't owe anybody anything. But he couldn't stop thinking about it. He had been taught that anybody who didn't bring him harm didn't deserve harm from his hands. Besides, firefighters were some of the only men in uniform Greg had respect for. They had shown up when the smoke rose from the Dawsons' rowhouse.

After these thoughts circled through in his mind for a few days, he decided he didn't regret what he'd done, but he wouldn't do it again. He decided that one day he'd make amends.

Jenny

O N WEDNESDAY, JENNY STARTED WRITING an email that
she would send the next day to the two people she knew
would understand how momentous the last five days of her life
had been.

From: Jenny Egan

Date: Thu, Apr 30, 2015 at 10:45 AM

Subject: The quick update

Hey Dad! Hey Rae!

Here's the update. I have NO voice right now but I have
fingers to type!
   The quick update is that I was contacted by the Ferguson Legal folks last week to see how they could help.
Over the weekend a group of about 15 of us set up a
legal team to run two major projects—legal observers and
jail support. Legal observers go out to all protests—not
to participate—but to observe and do cop watch. They

document techniques and if people get arrested, try to gather their names and contact information. They then call that information into jail support. At jail support—where I'm spending a lot of time—we are documenting arrests, methods, and connecting people with lawyers (either witnesses or arrestees). We also have people at the jail to greet people who are released, to document their injuries, to feed them, and to help them get home.

We started a bail fund—bails are outrageously high in Baltimore. They set $500K for one kid but routinely set $100K for misdemeanors. Just insane shit.

We are also running trainings for protestors and providing support. This is a black-led movement. My goal here is to amplify the voices of the black leaders and black protestors and to support their message—however they want to achieve it.

But I'm also a link to the public defender's office. I got us space in the office and have been helping to connect the major civil rights/lawyers to the local folks to coordinate briefs etc. We helped draft a habeas motion on Tuesday night when we realized the governor was saying he had the power to suspend the MD. rule that says you get a probable cause determination within 24 hours. We drafted that overnight, then the public defenders had people lined up to file as many motions as possible. We got 111 people released on state habeas yesterday. People will start filing federal habeas shortly.

As far as juveniles—they are scooping kids up without probable cause. And unlike adults, there is way more ways for them to justify it. I was doing emergency arraignments for kids on curfew violations (state asking to DETAIN) until 8 PM last night. Today looks just as bad.

Some big notes. One, an informant came to our very first meeting. I had to interrogate him after his answers didn't line up. Friendly, but strange. We had to ask him to leave. Pretty sure he was FBI as there are reports of him trying to infiltrate in Ferguson and other places previously. Whoa. That was day one, felt movie-like and surreal and it still sounds fake. But it was no joke.

I was at the Mondawmin Mall at 4:30 on Monday. The cops orchestrated that. They have a vested interest in discrediting the protests. Because they don't want reform and they don't want change. So there are usually 5,000 students that come through that bus stop every day. When the cops started putting out that there were "rumors" it was about 11 AM. THEN rumors did start and kids . . . stayed away. Cops say they confronted 75–100 kids. Teachers say that they UNLOADED buses of kids and then provoked those groups into a confrontation. There are videos of cops throwing rocks at kids. It's insane. But I'd love to hear how it was shown/perceived from far away.

I was at North & Pennsylvania later that night. Cops used an LRAD machine (this military grade weapon meant to disrupt your hearing). My ears still hurt and my throat is killing me. Assholes. It's illegal to use as a weapon, looking into drafting legal complaints about that. What else? Yesterday was tremendous. Students really coming together. The community is uniting against police and it's really beautiful to see. I mean—life changing great. I'm EXHAUSTED and emotionally wrung out, but also heartened.

In the end, the problem is that BPD is out of control. And it looks like they are learning nothing. Freddie Gray is dead because of a stop and arrest that lacked any probable cause whatsoever. And now they are running around in tanks, arresting people without any probable cause. I really believe that all people need to push state legislators to pass legislation that pushes back on the abusive practices the judiciary has allowed and promoted over the past 30 years. I'm hoping for some good legislation—across the country—to come out of this movement. But I also think this is going to be a years long struggle. I hope this is the moment. I hope Ferguson was the start and that five years from now we can celebrate a shift and a new civil rights movement in America.

I love you guys. If you were here, I know we'd be on the front lines together. You are both the reason I'm here doing what I'm doing. Thanks for being my role models and teaching me what it means to fight for justice.

Love you,
Jenny

Partee

W HEN PARTEE HAD COME HOME early Tuesday morning, his wife suggested to him—for the first time in their lives together—that maybe it was time to consider leaving the Baltimore City police. Cecelia deeply admired and respected the work of the force. But she was worried for her family's safety and sanity. Partee was close to a promotion to lieutenant colonel, which would represent a major step up and a signal accomplishment, but she couldn't help wondering if the police force in 2015 was different from the one she remembered growing up around—where the officers took care of each other, where "protect and serve" meant both the community and each other. She also wondered if Baltimore itself had changed irrevocably. She was a social worker, and they certainly needed his police force income, but she also wanted to make sure her husband was okay. "If it's bad, just come home," she said. "We will figure it out."

On Wednesday Partee walked into his district headquarters for the first time since Monday and was greeted cheerfully by his officers. He'd left the district late Monday morning to protect Mondawmin and was only now returning, two days later.

In that time, he had slept just a handful of hours, but he knew that he was not alone. His officers were all running on empty, too. He wanted to come in during the roll-call meeting, the daily meeting where all officers were accounted for and each shift was given instructions for the next twelve-hour period. Partee knew it was his job to protect the health and welfare of his officers, and right now he was worried about both. These had been five of the most trying days in the history of the city and its police department, and not a single one of his officers had called out sick or taken a medical day.

It was not just the commitment from his officers that impressed Partee. As he entered the district headquarters he was met by more than a hundred community members, all there to show their support. They included Orthodox Jewish leaders from Upper Park Heights and African American activists from Lower Park Heights. Rabbis and ministers. Children, parents, and grandparents.

The command center was full of people there to show gratitude to the officers for their work. They brought cases of water and baby wipes, Starbucks coffee, brown paper bags decorated with little blue stickers and full of snacks and chewing gum. They shook the hands of each of the officers and handed them a bottle of water, a spontaneous gathering organized by the community to wish them luck on their shift.

Partee was self-conscious as they hugged the community members, his white short-sleeved dress uniform stained, sweaty, and dusty from the military vehicles he was surrounded by all day down at the stadium. The uniform had seen better days— and so had Partee. But he teared up in the moment. The officers had seen so much over the past days, and everyone in the room knew that tough days still stared all of them in the face. But they were, at that moment, on the same team.

John

G AME DAY WAS OFTEN A sacred time for John. Everything that was done throughout the year is for this day. The trades, the coaching, the scouting, spring training—it's all for game day.

Normally on game day he was in constant motion, moving from the bleachers to the concession stands on the concourse and then over to the expensive boxes where wealthy execs and their guests dined on crab cakes and white wine instead of hot dogs and beer. He loved the looks on the faces of kids and their parents. He loved the familiar faces of the season ticket holders and the faces of the new fans who saved up all year for these three hours. He loved the concessions staff and ticket takers. The security guards and the groundskeepers. All of the people who proudly say they work for the Orioles, many of them from before the Angelos family even owned the team.

But today John was unsettled as he sat in his black leather chair with the word "Orioles" emblazoned in deep orange on the back. For the first time in baseball history, the game went on as time stood still.

His spacious office has a large window that offers views of the ballpark. John sat there, alone and in silence, but today his back faced the field as his beloved Orioles defended their empty house against their Chi-Town rivals. He'd decided that this was how he had to sit today, because there shouldn't be two sets of rules, as is often the case—one rule if you look a certain way, come from a certain family, are a certain color or sex, another rule for everyone else. So if the fans couldn't watch the game in person, neither would he.

A framed poster on the other wall of his office watched over him. It was from a Woody Guthrie celebration he'd attended. Guthrie, the famous American singer and songwriter, was known for his social justice songs. The words to one of those songs passed through John's head that day:

This land is your land, this land is my land
From California to the New York island
From the redwood forest to the Gulf Stream waters
This land was made for you and me

Tawanda

TAWANDA REALIZED ALMOST IMMEDIATELY THIS was not going to be a traditional West Wednesday. A weekly ritual since her brother's death, the average West Wednesday consisted of somewhere between one person and a dozen. The location of West Wednesday frequently changed. Sometimes it was in front of the Western District police station. Sometimes it was the congested corner of Thirty-third Street and Greenmount Avenue, right in the heart of commercial black Baltimore, near an Ace Hardware, a takeout steamed-crab spot, and a guy on the corner selling cellphone minutes. Sometimes it was by the site of Memorial Stadium, where the Orioles had once played, and where there was now a YMCA and senior housing. But today was different. She was going to go to the people whom she really wanted to hear her message. She was going to City Hall. And she was going to bring some friends with her.

Tawanda was using Facebook to communicate with people both about logistics and to help share the message about Tyrone. The death of Freddie and the subsequent unrest in Baltimore had brought fresh interest and attention to the issue of police violence. But this week was a turning point, and never again would she be on her own.

After work that day Tawanda had returned home to change from her conservative schoolteacher dress into a V-neck T-shirt that was Orioles orange. In the center of the shirt, in the same cursive lettering of the team logo, were the words "Tyrone West." She paired that with a black Orioles cap. Tawanda knew it was a little whimsical, but to her it made sense. Tyrone was her team. He was where her loyalty would forever lie.

She wept when she saw just how many people showed up for this West Wednesday. She'd never done this to draw big crowds. She wasn't a natural activist. She was simply a deter-mined sister. But today, with more than five hundred people standing in front of her, she felt validated. For years her West Wednesdays had been met with skeptical eyes and accusations of exaggeration and hyperbole. People admired her commit-ment but questioned her cause. But today they joined her. White faces, black faces, young faces, older faces. Baltimor-eans, Marylanders, others from around the country who had now been pulled in to join the cause. Even hip-hop legend Treach, the front man for the legendary 1990s group Naughty by Nature; she blushed because the rapper she'd had a teenage crush on was now telling her how much he admired her. Ev-eryone stood at the base of City Hall, looking toward the woman who spoke from its steps. They were hanging on her every word. She had all of them. And they all wanted to learn how they could help bring a peace to Tawanda that had been absent for years now, since her brother's death.

She informed the crowd that day that she was wearing this uniform because she found it interesting that a game was going on downtown, that sports in Baltimore had returned in an attempt to bring the city back to normalcy. Tawanda told the crowd that normalcy also meant that she would be out here every week until she got justice for her brother.

She'd been doing this so long and was tired, but the crowd reinvigorated her, giving her energy and a momentum she hadn't felt before. She spoke passionately to the audience in front of her: the supporters, the activists, other family members who sought justice for their loved ones. She fed off their support. She instructed them to be louder, to never stop demanding justice. For one man. Unarmed.

Epilogue

TAWANDA JONES

Tawanda Jones has not missed a week with West Wednesday, and to this day she still seeks justice for Tyrone. No one has been charged, arrested, or otherwise been held accountable for his death.

The state of Maryland rendered its verdict—the medical examiner said he'd died of cardiac arrhythmia complicated by dehydration during police restraint—and Tawanda spent the years after the riots challenging that answer.

Nearly one year to the day after the April 2015 riots, Tawanda got a different answer. An independent review of Tyrone's autopsy by pathologist Dr. William Manion concluded that Tyrone did not die of a heart condition. Manion wrote that Tyrone's death was a result of "positional asphyxia"—essentially, he had suffocated. But that April 2016 report still wasn't enough for the state's attorney to reopen the case.

A few months later, a forensic pathologist in Alabama was

willing to take another look at Tyrone's body, to see if he saw what she saw.

Tawanda spent $21,000 to have her brother's body ex-humed and sent down to Dr. Adel Shaker. Tawanda had re-searched him on the Internet. There was a story about how he had been able to determine that the cuts on a little girl's body that was found in the woods weren't from wildlife getting to her but had been deliberately inflicted.

Tawanda ran a tight operation, getting Tyrone's body sent down south, even sending a cousin to make sure that it was him lying on the table. Tyrone finally told his story. "West's cause of death is positional asphyxia, where he was not able to breathe during restraint process when he was held down by police officers sitting on him," Shaker wrote in the report, which was released at the end of 2016. He also wrote that re-straining West in a prone position while compromising his breathing was "the main cause of his demise."

In July, the city and state paid $1 million to settle a federal lawsuit filed by the West family in the aftermath of Tyrone's death. The family had alleged police misconduct and use of excessive force. But Tawanda removed herself as a plaintiff so that the money could go to Tyrone's children—and so that she could be free from a non-disparagement agreement that would have silenced her, prevented her from speaking the words that continue to ring out in Baltimore every Wednesday.

"One man. Unarmed."

JENNY EGAN

Jenny Egan continues to fight for children.

After the uprising, she stayed in her role as a juvenile public defender, but her newfound friends from the days of the riots

founded a new grassroots legal service, called the Baltimore
Action Legal Team (BALT). The team provides legal support
to Baltimore communities who exercise their civil liberties
protesting against injustices rooted in structural racism and
economic inequality.

Since then, BALT has helped coordinate legal and jail
support for protests, including the #Afromation protest at
Artscape, sit-ins at City Hall, and various other actions around
the city. They also have partnered on a successful Mama's Day
Bail Out program and now are building a community lawyer
brain trust to connect volunteer lawyers to Baltimore organizations and communities who need legal information and
input.

Other volunteers from the uprising's legal circle have created spin-offs. At the University of Baltimore Law School
there is now a thriving National Lawyers Guild chapter that
runs a legal observation program, a group that provides jail
support every week to recently released folks at BCDC. Jenny
said that as a result of the riots, there is now a community
lawyer brain trust to connect volunteer lawyers to Baltimore
organizations and communities that need legal information
and input.

"There is infrastructure now for protest and for holding the
city accountable for unconstitutional behavior that did not
exist in 2015," Jenny said.

Jenny's also seen a change in her office, a reinvigoration of
the culture. "Baltimore defenders have long seen their clients
beat up, harassed, illegally detained, and even murdered by police not just without accountability but without concern or
care from the media or the public," she said. "When people you
invest in and care about are abused and no one bats an eye, it
can leave you jaded and hopeless. When you jump and scream

and yell—and the prosecutors, the police, and the bench do nothing to stop the abuse of your clients—it can drain the fight out of you. When Baltimore stood up and spoke out for Freddie, the fact that our city yelled so loud the whole world heard us say no meant defenders didn't feel like they were fighting in complete darkness anymore."

But the light only flickers, Jenny said. Three people died in BCDC in 2018, including a mentally ill man who was there on a traffic violation, and no one has paid attention or held anyone accountable.

Jenny also believes that a scene she saw at the end of the April 27 uprising led to one of the most impactful accountability measures seen in the history of the Baltimore Police Department. When she saw a white man run out of the CVS, the hair on Jenny's arms stood up. She thought he was a plant, an agent provocateur. "That dude is a cop!" she yelled out. After she identified him, he was chased by a group of protesters to his car, the only one left in a parking lot outside of CVS. The man tripped, and somebody gave him a gentle kick in the butt before he managed to get himself to the door of his black late-model sedan, with no plates on the front. Jenny watched as he got in and screeched toward the police line that had formed toward North Avenue. She was startled when she watched the police line part to let him through and he just drove away.

Three years later, it was revealed that one officer of an elite squad called the Gun Trace Task Force was in possession of trash bags of prescription drugs looted from pharmacies during the riots that he intended to resell.

GREG BUTLER

In the days after the uprising, Greg Butler sat in jail as law enforcement hunted for the man in the gas mask. When he was arrested he had given them an alias, Greg Bailey, and days went by before they figured it out. They put a picture of the gas-mask-wearing man out on the news, labeling him a wanted individual. And they offered a reward, too. Greg was surprised that he hadn't been turned in by someone from his neighborhood who needed the money. In the meantime, Greg Bailey—the man police found entering a looted store and attempting to steal cigarettes—was charged with second-degree escape, possession of a dangerous weapon with intent to injure, and attempted theft of less than $100. A few days later Greg Butler was confirmed as the infamous man behind the gas mask who had cut the fire hose. He was charged with malicious destruction of property, reckless endangerment, and obstructing firefighters.

Greg was held without bail for the next month awaiting trial, and a jury found him guilty but offered him probation. His freedom was short-lived, however. Greg knew that he had an audience at his state trial, the men who sat in the back of the courtroom in dark jackets and followed him to the bathroom and outside to smoke a cigarette. As soon as he left the courtroom from his first trial, they moved in to arrest him on federal charges.

At his trial, prosecutors and his attorney had litigated his whole life—the life of a black Baltimore boy who, no matter how much he tries to stay out of trouble, winds up with it finding him anyway. In the end, after he pleaded guilty, he addressed US District Court judge J. Frederick Motz about his state of mind that day: "I was lost. Everything fell south on me. I didn't feel like I had family I could turn to. I felt lonely when basketball wasn't there for me anymore. It was going to be the way out. And when that door closed, I panicked, and that panic showed through my actions." More important than his past, he said, he had a future, a son.

Among those who spoke on Greg's behalf, a surprise witness presented himself: Robert Maloney, Baltimore's director of emergency management, who sought him out after he heard of the standout basketball star turned "menace."

"I wanted to meet him, and I wanted to hear from him why he did what he did, and I wanted to figure out where in the hell he got an old gas mask from that day given no one else had one on, and how he ended up on the cover of *Time* magazine," Maloney said.

Through conversations, Maloney said, he learned not only about Greg but about his city. "I learned a lot about him, and I, like others, have taken the choice to help him to get him on track, and so I've done that in phone conversations and just seeing what he's up to, and thinking about future employment—I know he has some college background—channeling that. I know he's a father now. And so my perception of all of this in this particular case—and nothing has changed my mind that I've heard today—is that sending him to federal prison is not going to help him or us."

Prosecutors were seeking charges that carried mandatory minimums: aiding and abetting arson, which would require twenty years, and obstructing firefighting, which required a minimum of five. His attorneys argued that the charges were excessive, particularly for a victimless crime. If convicted, he would have been one of several arrestees who served more time than any of the police officers who were charged in the death of Freddie.

But Greg ended up with three years of supervised release and 250 hours of community service, and he was ordered to pay $1 million in restitution. "There have been enough victims," Judge Motz told Greg. "I don't want to make you another victim." For his community service, Greg volunteered with the fire department, helped with his neighborhood mentoring program, and was tapped to serve on the mayor's youth council, all while working seven days a week.

Greg felt that he had a new lease on life, though after his release he could not escape some of his demons. He violated parole and fell behind on his restitution payments. "I'm not asking for too much, just a chance to get back in the fight," he told the judge in court.

Today, Greg is thriving. He is living with his two children and fiancée in Baltimore, serves as a mentor to young children, and works as an assistant dean and girls' basketball coach at a public charter school. His father died in November 2017. He and his mother, who is now clean, have a strong relationship. His probation was scheduled to end at the end of 2019.

ANTHONY WILLIAMS

The financial woes that seemed to strike Shake & Bake after the death of Freddie Gray never eased; in fact, they got worse. By the close of 2015, Shake & Bake's annual revenue was down almost 60 percent from the year before. Even when the numbers didn't pick up and people urged Anthony to lay people off, he refused. He knew that the young people who worked for him didn't have a lot of options outside of the Shake & Bake. Keeping the staff on was an additional strain in a time of reduced revenue.

In August 2017, Anthony Williams circled the halls of

Shake & Bake, peeling posters off the walls and putting them in the boxes that would contain the last of his legacy there. The city had decided that it was time for Shake & Bake to move on without Anthony as the general manager, firing him after decades of work. It was also going to shut the Bake down and "refurbish" it for an unannounced and undetermined grand reopening. An institution that had been a Baltimore fixture for thirty years was closing. Anthony wept as he locked the doors for the final time, feeling like the most important chapter in his life had been rewritten for him, taken from him when he had nothing else to hold on to.

About a month after the closing, on September 24, 2017, Malik was shot and killed right across the street from Shake & Bake. When Anthony had seen him two months earlier, Malik was holding a bottle of Patrón tequila, his eyes drooping and reddened. "You're changing," Anthony told him, heartbroken at seeing his mentee take such a turn for the worse. So when Anthony got word about the shooting, he was more grief-stricken than surprised. As their motto said, Shake & Bake saves lives. And when it was gone, lives were lost.

A year later, in March 2018, after ordering the closing of Shake & Bake, the new mayor was in attendance when it reopened. "When I shut it down you would have thought that I shut down heaven," she said. "When I shut it down my phone blew up like a fire engine." Glenn "Shake & Bake" Doughty, the former Baltimore Colts player whom Shake & Bake was named after, stood there smiling as the doors opened in front of a crowd. Anthony didn't attend; in fact, he wasn't invited. He watched the evening news recap of smiling faces and kids with skates on from his small home in Towson.

NICK MOSBY

On Friday, May 1, Nick Mosby raced to City Hall to see if the rumors were true—that his wife was standing at the War Memorial Building announcing a litany of charges against the six officers who had arrested Freddie Gray. Nobody expected to hear from her so quickly after the police completed their report and submitted it to the state attorney's office. But on Friday afternoon, Marilyn Mosby uttered words that shocked the world, words that many who had been protesting had been waiting to hear: "The findings of our comprehensive, thorough, and independent investigation, coupled with the medical examiner's determination that Mr. Gray's death was a homicide, which we received today, has led us to believe that we have probable cause to file criminal charges." With those words, the six officers under investigation for the death of Freddie Gray were now indicted and would be soon awaiting trials for the role they'd played in the death of the young man. These were the first indictments of police officers in the death of civilians ever in Baltimore, and instantaneously made Marilyn Mosby a hero in many communities of color and a pariah in many chapters of the Fraternal Order of Police.

Six months after the riots, Nick Mosby stood in Reservoir Hill, his wife and a crowd of supporters behind him, and announced that he would run for mayor. Having been a City Council member since 2011, he was finally pursuing his lifelong dream, and he laid out his plans for revitalizing a city. The incumbent, Stephanie Rawlings-Blake, had announced weeks before that she would not seek reelection.

The race was crowded, with fifteen people declaring their candidacies: along with Nick, they included Baltimore's former mayor Sheila Dixon; Elizabeth Embry, attorney and daughter of a former Baltimore City Council member; long-time City Council member Carl Stokes; and activist DeRay Mckesson all ran spirited races. In April 2016, weeks before election day, Mosby announced that he was dropping out of the race and would back the eventual winner, State Sen. Catherine Pugh, who won by fewer than two percentage points. Considering the upheaval and opportunity for change, the turnout was categorically low, with only 45 percent of registered Baltimoreans turning out.

Eventually, Nick was appointed as a delegate to the Maryland legislature, serving as a representative for the district he lives in and loves.

MARC PARTEE

Following the unrest of April 27, 2015, Baltimore saw an unprecedented spike in homicides. Some blamed it on the flow of new pharmaceutical drugs on the street following the looting from the drugstores. Some blamed it on the belief that many police officers, now feeling they would be prosecuted, stopped policing certain areas and allowed crimes to take place there. Some blamed it on an overwhelmed City Hall. Some thought it was a combination of all of these reasons. But 2015 ended with Baltimore recording 344 murders, the second-highest number in Baltimore history—the only year with more had been 1993, when the population was 100,000 higher.

On July 8, 2015, Police Commissioner Anthony Batts was fired from the Baltimore Police Department in the aftermath of the spike in homicides. But Partee's confrontation with Batts had real implications for Partee's career, too. Once seen as a rising star in the department, Partee's career stalled, and despite a notable record, he was passed over for promotion to lieutenant colonel. In September 2015, he was tapped by the new police commissioner to lead the training academy, a position not seen as a fast-track job in the police force but one he took on with excitement. He saw it as an opportunity to shape the future of the police force—and the city. Recruitment was down significantly, with fewer people applying to be police officers; Partee had to deal with a 14 percent drop in cadets and new officers. One of the big changes that Partee instituted was significantly increasing the Mobile Field Force Training, or riot control training.

His oldest son became a weightlifting champion and wanted to join the Baltimore police force. His father told him no. He ended up joining the navy instead, where he is serving.

Partee eventually retired from the Baltimore City Police Force after twenty-two years on the job. He was named the director of public safety and chief of police for Lincoln University, a historically black college in Pennsylvania.

JOHN ANGELOS

The challenges Baltimore has experienced have also coincided with changes in the Orioles' fortunes. A once-promising team full of All-Stars and consistently mentioned for a deep playoff run has fallen into rebuilding mode, with top stars leaving. After winning the American League East in 2014—one of the most competitive divisions in baseball, as it includes the high-powered and high-payroll Boston Red Sox and New York Yankees—the Orioles' slide has been real and consistent. By 2016, the Orioles tumbled to third place in the division, and by 2018, with a winning percentage of .290, they were now one of the losingest teams in baseball.

Attendance at the games also took a significant dip. The

Orioles have had losing streaks before, but getting Baltimoreans into the seats to either cheer or boo had not been an issue until recently. Attendance at the Orioles games since the uprising has been down close to 40 percent, with the combination of team performance and perceived downtown safety taking a toll on the organization's promise and profitability. Creative incentives to get people into the ballpark as well as rethinking the relationship with the community have been distinct priorities. Gone are the ribbon-cuttings and construction of swing sets; a deeper-rooted engagement with the community is the new core philanthropic effort. The idea is to get the players to be *of* Baltimore and not simply *in* Baltimore.

John and his brother, Louis, also saw increasing responsibilities with the team as the health of their father, Peter Angelos, declined. And the lawsuit with the Washington Nationals over MASN now stretches into its seventh year.

BILLY MURPHY

In the fall of 2015, the Gray family and the city of Baltimore finally settled. The finalized terms granted the Gray family a $6.4 million payout, with Freddie's mother, Gloria, receiving $5.36 million and Freddie's father, who had no real connection with Freddie until his death, receiving $640,000. Since the Freddie Gray case, Billy has represented several hundred other plaintiffs in cases involving police brutality or excessive police force. Billy was also instrumental in the 2016 consent decree between the city of Baltimore and the US Department of Justice. His sister, who worked for US attorney general Loretta Lynch, worked closely with Billy to craft the case that led to the final decision. The consent decree mandated sweeping police reforms after a Department of Justice investigation found widespread discriminatory policing in the city, particularly in poor black neighborhoods. Hundreds of incidents were publicly uncovered. The decree requires restrictions on police officers and how they engage individuals suspected of criminal activity, and also requires the police department to enhance officer training and accountability. Almost immediately after the Trump administration took office, the consent decree was put under review, with then–Attorney General Jeff Sessions saying he had "grave concerns that some of the provisions of the decree will reduce the lawful powers of the police department and result in a less safe city." Billy has been a vocal advocate for the consent decree to make sure true accountability comes to Baltimore. He continues to travel the country urging for criminal justice reform, and he continues to stay in touch with the Gray family.

BALTIMORE

Perhaps no character came out of the 2015 riots worse off or more divided than Baltimore.

In the days after the riots, the Baltimore state's attorney, Marilyn Mosby, announced that she would charge six officers in the death of Freddie Gray. In the May 1 announcement, Mosby came down the stairs of the War Memorial Building to declare that she was heeding the calls of "No justice, no peace." Months later, none of the officers had been convicted, and there has not been peace in Baltimore since.

In the months after the April 2015 unrest, the city devolved into what law enforcement and citizens alike described as consistent unrest. Resentful and fearful of prosecution, some police stopped protecting and serving. Arrests plummeted in May to the lowest percentages seen in any month for at least

three years, according to city arrest data, as officers began
turning a blind eye to drug dealing, robberies in broad day-
light, and routine violations.

By then, the national news outlets had disappeared, the politicians had gone back to day-to-day business, and the prom-
ises of change that had echoed through the city for one hopeful
week went unfulfilled. The programs for youth, whose clash
with officers sparked the unrest, were not adequately sustained, and many withered under financial pressure. The
neighborhood blight that served as a backdrop for interviews
about Baltimore's impending renaissance still showed disre-
pair. The streets were still hosting gun battles and bloodbaths.

Mayor Stephanie Rawlings-Blake announced she would not
seek reelection. Residents chose longtime Baltimore state sen-
ator Catherine Pugh to go to City Hall, and along with a fresh
slate of City Council members, Baltimore appeared ready for a
new start. But by 2017, the homicide rate surged, and Baltimore logged 342 murders—the highest rate in its history, and
the highest of any major city in the country. That same year,
the Baltimore Police Department delivered another blow to an
already battered city: the largest corruption case in its history.
Eight officers were indicted on federal racketeering charges,
including robberies, extortion, and other crimes that unleashed unfettered terror on the city. The elite unit of the Gun
Trace Task Force was also believed to have been among the
traffickers of drugs stolen from a burning CVS and dozens of
other looted pharmacies during the riots, contributing to a
violent crime spike in the city in the days and weeks after
Gray's funeral.

As the officers went on trial, a key witness walked into an
alleyway and was later found gravely wounded in a vacant lot
by a bullet shot from his own gun. It was revealed that the

victim, Baltimore City police detective Sean Suiter, was scheduled to testify before a grand jury in the Gun Trace Task Force
case the day after the shooting. The state medical examiner
ruled his death a homicide, but an independent panel later determined that evidence supported the conclusion that he took
his own life. His family told *The Baltimore Sun* that they believed it was an "inside job."

Suiter's death and the surrounding mystery and conspiracy
shook the scant confidence the city had that it had reached a
turning point. And just when it seemed things couldn't get
any worse, they did. In 2019, the *Sun* published a series of
damning articles about self-dealing board members at the
University of Maryland Medical System. One of the worst of-
fenders: Baltimore mayor Catherine Pugh. She resigned in dis-
grace on May 2, and in November 2019 she was indicted on
eleven counts, including fraud, tax evasion, and conspiracy.

Author's Note 2020

WRITING THIS BOOK HAS BEEN a four-year pursuit of two fundamental questions: What really happened over those five days? And what do we do next?

I chose eight stories to represent the ways the events of April 2015 drew in people in every stratum of the city. I am so grateful to each of them for spending so much time and investing their emotional and intellectual labor in this project. I have tried to honor their lived experience and draw insight and inspiration from their stories.

But I want to spend the last moments of this book trying to listen to the one voice I never got to hear. Freddie Gray is the reason these lives intersected in the way that they did. What does his life—and how it ended—tell us, the living, about what happened during those five days and why? What does it tell us about what we do next?

Freddie's short life underscores a dramatic truth: wealth and income inequality define modern American life. Millions of children are condemned to lives that are shorter, less healthy, and with fewer opportunities by virtue of their zip code and, often, the color of their skin. They live in hypersegregated, intensely impoverished neighborhoods, created and reinforced by a web of policies, systems, and institutions. In 2019, in the United States, 9.6 million children lived in poverty. A bipartisan, congressionally mandated study by the National Academy of Sciences estimated that child poverty costs the country between $800 billion and $1.1 trillion every year in lost adult productivity, increased costs related to crime, and increased health expenditures. As staggering as that number is, it fails to capture the untapped genius and unrealized potential of these nearly ten million American children trapped in poverty. Some critics will counter that poverty is a choice made by those who are lazy or who lack the desire to change their lives for the better. I agree that poverty is a choice. But that choice is not made by the people who live under its oppressive effects. Rather, the choice is ours. It's the choice of the government that represents our priorities and allocates our investments. It's a choice reinforced by the companies we patronize and the organizations we support.

For Freddie, and the millions like him, the hardship and the obstacles began in the womb. From birth through the early years of her adult life, Freddie's mother, Gloria, lived in poverty and battled heroin addiction. Gloria never attended high school and could not read or write. Young, vulnerable, sick, and alone, Gloria delivered Freddie and his twin sister two months premature. The twins spent their first months of life in a hospital unit. While their basic survival needs were met, they were far from nurtured. Instead, from birth, Freddie and his sister endured neglect with lifelong consequences. We know that children who are institutionalized at birth and receive limited or rationed adult contact are more likely to suffer severe impairments in cognitive, physical, and psychosocial development.

The neglect that Freddie experienced at birth would transform into negligence throughout his childhood. There is an unhelpful narrative that people like Freddie Gray somehow deserve what happens to them. That, if Freddie were living his life the right way, then he would not have had that encounter with the police in April 2015. However, every meaningful data point about Freddie points to how he was brought into this world and then how the world treated him, repeatedly and ruthlessly, throughout his life. From his mother's untreated addiction to lead poisoning to failed schools, we chose Freddie's destiny for him.

American rates of deep poverty are unmatched in the developed world. And while spending on federal welfare programs has increased relative to levels of the 1980s, the majority of those resources have not reached the deeply impoverished. This is by design. In America, help from society is closely indexed to your ability to work. Those disconnected from the labor market—like Freddie's mother and later Freddie himself—are largely excluded from the societal safety net. Consider that "three decades ago, the poorest families in America received most (56%) of the transfers going to families with private incomes below 200% of the federal poverty threshold; in recent years, those families received less than one-third of the transfers," according to poverty scholar Robert Moffitt. Our society's insistence on limiting help to those who "deserve it," as indicated by their status in the labor market, has a profound impact on the capacity of those living in deep poverty to escape. We should be encouraging work and doing more to support those who make up the majority of those living in poverty in our country, the working poor. We must end the inhumane debate about who are the deserving versus the undeserving poor.

Our increasing tolerance of deep poverty and the nearly permanent underclass it has created in America is dramatically reshaping our country. A recent study by the OECD compared economic mobility among its member states. The study found that a person born into a low-income family in the United States would need *five generations* to reach the mean household income in the country. Over the last half century, the American Dream—simply put, doing better than your parents—has become a coin flip for most Americans. Freddie's hardship began before he was born because his mother's life was, in many ways, as haunted as his own. Gloria's own poverty, lack of education, and battles with drug addiction were the foundation of her children's lives. When we fail to address poverty in one generation, that poverty will more than likely extend indefinitely, generation after generation.

When we take an inventory of major policy action over the last few years, we see policy makers doing little to benefit or change the opportunities available to low- or even middle-income families. The federal tax cuts created by the 2017 Tax Cuts and Jobs Act (TCJA) are largely tilted toward high-income households and foreign investors. In 2018, 70 percent of tax cuts under TCJA accrued to the top 20 percent of taxpayers. Working Americans saw little benefit. And Americans living in poverty experienced absolutely no change.

If our systems for wealth preservation and creation—the tax code, the banking system, investment markets, the labor market—excluded Freddie Gray entirely, other systems intentionally captured him, literally. Freddie spent most of his adult life under some form of correctional control. He was not alone. Black Americans constitute 13 percent of the population but represent 35 percent of the population touched by the criminal justice system. For many black Americans, their experience with criminal justice forecloses work, housing, and other avenues that might lead to stability. The stigma and lifelong negative bias that result from even a fleeting encounter with the criminal justice system are absolutely life-changing. In Freddie's case, those encounters directly led to his death. The same was true of Tamir Rice. And Sandra Bland. And Eric Garner. And the list goes on.

If we permit these tragedies to recede from memory, we risk missing the opportunity to change the systems ultimately responsible for these injustices. Which brings me back to the questions that drove this project: What happened? And what can change? The figures in this book were each, in their way, fighting to prevent the tragedy of Freddie Gray from playing out again and again. Some tried to change the system from the ground up, working in their communities. This is the story of Tawanda, Anthony, and Greg. Others attempted to fight injustice from positions of privilege. John Angelos is one such example. Others, like Nick, Jenny, Marc, and Billy, worked from inside the system. In their small victories and looming failures, they revealed to me the importance of individual changemakers *and* the indispensable necessity of collective action.

Tawanda, Anthony, and Greg call our attention to the ways systemic injustice is not just an abstraction but can permeate our everyday lives. Tawanda's work highlights how the criminal justice system affects more than the men whose lives are irrevocably changed when they encounter the system. It's important to note that the Black Lives Matter movement—which calls attention, among other things, to the fatal impact of policing on black men—was founded by black women. Anthony personifies the importance of recognizing the unsupported assets that anchor communities struggling under the grind of deep poverty. If Tawanda calls our attention to the oppression endemic in our communities, Anthony lifts up what's hopeful. If Tawanda demands that we petition the state, Anthony reminds us to work *within* the community to serve the state's constituents. In the midst of crisis, Anthony didn't wait for others to help. He acted, he served. That fateful Tuesday, when Anthony, on his day off, observed the young girl cleaning the streets following a day of protests, Anthony did what he knew to do: he showed up, he went to work. Tawanda's steadfast protest and Anthony's sense of community duty are inspiring, but we should resist the idea that good deeds are sufficient to lead us out of the darkness. In many ways, they both spend their lives cleaning up debris that results from a broken system. And they deserve better.

Greg Butler's story personifies the dilemma that confronts many black men in the United States who are "lucky enough to make it out." No doubt Greg was lucky, having escaped an early death to get a shot at a quality education and athletic career. But the trauma from early childhood and the lack of assets surrounding Greg into his adulthood—a stable family, for instance—made it almost impossible for him to sustain his escape. Obstacles like an unpaid college bill that would never derail a middle-class or affluent young person short-circuited Greg's progress. Greg's story teaches us that the work isn't finished when someone gets a job or an education; our commitment to and investment in the most vulnerable has to extend beyond those first steps. By the time Greg cuts the fire hose, we see that his built-up frustration wasn't about anger at the fire department, it was questioning whether the city should be saved at all. As an African proverb states, a child who is not embraced by the village will burn it down to feel the fire's warmth.

What does the pursuit of change look like from the halls of power and privilege? John Angelos was born into enormous privilege and badly wanted to leverage his position for good. John truly and genuinely cares about people, especially the dispossessed. On the first night of the unrest, John became notorious for tweets underscoring the vast discrepancies in opportunity that led to that fateful week in April. There weren't many people in his position speaking up with such clarity and urgency. But it's important to acknowledge that John obviously has less at stake than others profiled in the book. John's wealth and position of power were useful in this case, but in a more significant way, that kind of wildly disproportionate wealth exemplifies the problem. John was at the center of the decision to play the baseball game with no fans because he wanted to draw the world's attention to the gross disparities on display in Baltimore that week. John's actions also underscore the limits of symbolic gestures toward social justice that we also often see in the world of philanthropy. We pay homage to what needs to change and attempt half measures, but we rarely challenge our own complicity in the structural inequities. For that reason, dramatic and badly needed change remains out of reach. We rely on our philanthropic prowess to cover as best we can for the structural deficiencies. And while philanthropic impact and truly generous and human giving are applauded and necessary in the United States, there is not enough philanthropy in the world to exclusively address the disparities that exist. Figure this: Every year, approximately $700 billion goes toward philanthropy. That is a large and real number. Now, approximately half of it goes to colleges and universities, building endowments that can end up in the tens of billions (for example, the endowment at Harvard University is $36 billion). And of the remaining $350 billion in philanthropy, half goes toward hospitals and houses of worship. So now there is approximately $175 billion left over. For everything else. The environment. Animals. Support for seniors. For veterans returning home from war. Education. Housing. Brain development. Immigrant support. Global health. Economic injustice.

Philanthropy can and should be catalytic. I proudly run what is by all measures one of the most quantifiably effective philanthropies in the country, yet our truth is while our philanthropy is catalytic and individually important, our strength is in using our capital to create scale of impact. To take good ideas and powerful models that we can fund and be obsessive about turning them into systemic change. I do not run a charity. I don't believe in that. I run a change organization. Being a change organization means being aggressive yet humble about the change we are hoping to elicit. It means working in deliberate concert with all leadership pillars of society, public, private, philanthropic, and the People, to create long-lasting and measurable metamorphosis.

Throughout the book, we witness Jenny, Marc, and Nick, in their own ways, laboring from within the system to change things for the better. Jenny's story testifies to the importance of understanding the humanity that is overlooked by our systems of opportunity and justice. Marc Partee worked hard to help the police live up to their higher aspirations and engage the community on their terms. However, the police force and its political leaders did not have the resources or strategies needed to address a pain that was much deeper than one that was their making alone, or to defuse the crisis and move the city forward. Marc's work, however admirable, was not enough, and he ultimately paid the price for speaking up and trying to change things from the inside. Nick Mosby also penetrated the system and tried to change it, only to encounter paralysis. The tool of government, as it's structured, is simply not up to the task of changing the fundamental dynamics that condemn our communities. "Throw the bums out" and "Drain the swamp" are popular political slogans. But it's not enough to move people around in a bureaucracy if you don't change the underlying values and let those values reshape tactics and procedures. Billy Murphy delivers an almost Old Testament sense of justice to Freddie Gray and his family by extracting a modicum of restitution from a profoundly broken system. But that doesn't change the clear lesson: without structural change, even good people will hit a wall. The challenges are far too entrenched and our individual tools are too limited.

So how do we move forward? Our collective pursuit of justice must be as aggressive and intentional as the systemwide injustice that we now encounter. We must alter how we define the state and permanence of poverty. We must acknowledge and challenge our own complicity. And we must put forward policies that actively confront the systematic bias of past policies.

We call those living with the scourge of poverty "poor people," as if it's a title of choice, but it can become a phrase that gives permission to ignore someone's humanity. Poverty is a condition our society does not have to tolerate or condone. "Poor people" signifies permanence. A birthright. Similar to the term "slave," as if that's what the individual was born to achieve. Slavery is a man-made inhumanity. A human mandate. Enslaved people are victims of the institution of slavery. The resilient souls living in poverty are victims of the institution of poverty. We cannot be true allies if we see our mandate

as being saviors of a few deserving "poor people." Everyone's
destinies matter.

Our country has a long history, and for much of it the intentional policy of the United States was to create hierar-
chies of people based on their class, race, and gender. We live
with that legacy today, and it is an undeniable undercurrent
in our politics. We need to formally and diligently examine
the causes and traumas of generational economic inequality
and their intersection with issues of race, gender, national
origin, and sexuality. We have examples of nations that have
stared into their deepest wounds and emerged stronger. In
the late twentieth century, South Africa, Chile, and Northern
Ireland, among others, all convened commissions dedicated
to truth and reconciliation. Those commissions created a di-
alogue about the harm done in their communities across generations, much of it rooted in bigotry and demagoguery, and
presented a path forward to better policies and the political
solidarity needed to enact them. In 2015, Canada completed a
seven-year process in which the Truth and Reconciliation
Commission of Canada uncovered the history of the Canadian
Indian residential school system and its lasting impacts on in-
digenous students and their families. The survivors had a
chance to have their pain heard. The perpetrators had a chance
to share their sorrow and apologies. Canada had a chance to
begin the healing process. These processes have not been perfect and the aftermath in the respective nations has not come
without false starts and setbacks, but that did not mean they
stopped pushing for progress. This level of national courage is
important. We individually must initiate our own truth and
reconciliation process, in each of us, in our own hearts and
communities. We must wrestle with the history of complicity
and bias, and work to address these disparities. As Americans,

we have a sacred responsibility to eliminate the myth and frequent talking point "It happened so long ago" or "Why am I being punished for what my ancestors did?" Our complicity in the ongoing harm unfolding in our neighborhoods and those of our neighbors is the surest way to guarantee that our country will not change for the better.

To be clear, we understand poverty—its impacts, its causes, and its corollaries—better than at any point in human history. Which means action is a pure question of will. Entire books can be written, and have been, on things we can and should do to promote increasing pathways and opportunities around education, housing, transportation, and health, among other priorities. The aforementioned study, for example, that estimated the costs of child poverty annually hovering around $1 trillion also provided a clear and compelling road map for cutting child poverty in half in the next decade. The report recommended a combination of work supports for parents and the expansion of supports for children, like SNAP (the Supplemental Nutrition Assistance Program), to alleviate the worst of child poverty in the United States. This would require investment, but it's far from onerous: our federal government spent more than $4 trillion in 2018. Cutting child poverty in half would cost roughly $100 billion a year, a significant figure but still only a bit more than 2 percent of our federal budget. Furthermore, the dividends from that investment would extend far beyond a dramatic decrease in child poverty; adults would see a dramatic increase in their earnings in real time and the lifetime prospects of the children lifted out of poverty would be meaningfully and durably improved. Additionally, we know there are few impacts as pernicious and unrelenting on the development and life prospects of people than lead poisoning. Lead poisoning is a nationwide and preventable crisis, affecting children in urban, rural, and suburban contexts. Lead's neurotoxic impacts are color-blind and class-blind, but the urgency to remedy them oftentimes is not.

A 2018 report by the Pew Charitable Trusts estimated that addressing lead-based paint hazards in the homes of low-income children would deliver $3.5 billion in future benefits. Addressing and removing leaded drinking water service lines from only the homes of children born in 2018 would protect more than 350,000 children from lead exposure and yield an estimated $2.7 billion in future benefits. If we addressed lead poisoning across the country, we would do more than protect the future for hundreds of thousands of vulnerable children— we would save ourselves billions of dollars of future costs for special education and behavioral health, as well as juvenile and criminal justice costs. We would create billions of dollars in value from higher high school graduation rates and the lifetime earnings from these lives we cast aside when they're only children.

The pride and promise of America are too strong to allow our scattered past to hinder its prospects. Loving your country means fighting for the institutionalization of its core goodness. Loving your country does not mean lying about its past. Loving your country means learning and embracing the history of those who fought for her, even when she didn't always reflect the same level of courageousness or allegiance in return.

It's our time to use our individual voices, power, will, and privilege to address economic injustice. To fight for those who have been consistently left out. Pay homage to those who worked tirelessly to clean and fix houses, roads, and bridges that they were not allowed to live in or travel on. Those who built economies that they could not participate in. Those who were repeatedly asked to be patient, told that the American story would include them, but never saw their place in line advance. Those who were unknowingly writing the American story, but were never acknowledged as authors. Understand that the best way to protect our own future is to protect the future of others. To use our power to demand justice. We aren't asking that everyone end up in the same spot. We are asking that everyone get a fair shot. Not selective misery and judicious pathways, but true channels where destiny can be determined and not predetermined. Where poverty does not have to be a preordination. Where pain does not have to be predictable. Where promise can be promised. Like the lives of our eight protagonists over five days, our fates are profoundly intertwined.

Notes on Sources

THE EVENTS IN THIS BOOK were recounted and reconstructed based largely on interviews with the eight subjects. Supplemental interviews were conducted with Baltimore City residents, political leaders, law enforcement officials, and social justice activists. We reviewed court records and transcripts, public records and data, and social media accounts of Baltimore media outlets and activists. We also used extensive news coverage to prepare for interviews, for research and reporting, and to confirm facts, details, and interviewee accounts. Notable citations that contributed to reporting include, but are not limited to:

Coverage of the death of Freddie Gray and protests, *The Baltimore Sun, Baltimore City Paper, The Guardian*; Sheridan Merrick, "The Story of Tyrone West, and the Sister Who Keeps Fighting for Justice," *Odyssey*; coverage of the death of Anthony Anderson, *The Baltimore Sun*, WMAR (page 5); "The Counted: People Killed by Police in the U.S.," *The Guardian* (page 8); Kevin Rector, Twitter account (page 18, Malik Shabazz quote "Let's shake it up at this baseball game"); Baynard Woods, "Baltimore Officers Cited for Mistreatment of Women in DoJ Report," *The Guardian* (page 37);

Encyclopedia of the Great Plains, edited by David J. Wishart, University of Nebraska–Lincoln (page 72, description of Okies); Erica L. Green, "School Board to Review Weighted GPAs," *The Baltimore Sun* (page 114); Luke Broadwater, "Police: Man Falls to His Death in Chase," *Washington Examiner* (page 198); Mary Wiltenburg and Mary Rose Madden, "Running from Cops," *Reveal/WYPR* (page 198); Juliet Linderman, "New Autopsy: Man in Police Struggle Died of Asphyxiation," Associated Press (page 234, description of Tyrone West autopsy, "He also wrote that restraining West in a prone position while compromising his breathing was 'the main cause of his demise,'" Tawanda Epilogue); Rick Ritter, "Baltimore Man Gets Supervised Release for Slicing Fire Hose During Riots," CBS Baltimore (page 238, Greg Epilogue); Baynard Woods, "Tale of Two Baltimores: Why Freddie Gray Protester May Face Tougher Sentence Than Officer on Trial," *The Guardian* (page 238, "If convicted, he would have been one of several arrestees who served more time than any of the police officers who were charged in the death of Freddie," Greg Epilogue); Doug Donovan and Colin Campbell, "Arrests in Baltimore Plummet, and Residents Are Fearful," *The Baltimore Sun* (page 245, "Arrests plummeted in May to the lowest percentages seen in any month for at least three years," Baltimore Epilogue); Brad Heath, "Baltimore Police Stopped Noticing Crime After Freddie Gray's Death. A Wave of Killings Followed," *USA Today* (page 246, "blind eye to . . . routine violations," Baltimore Epilogue); Alec MacGillis, "The Tragedy of Baltimore," *The New York Times*/ProPublica (page 246, "Baltimore logged 342 murders—the highest rate in its history, and the highest of any major city in the country," Baltimore Epilogue); coverage of the death of Sean Suiter/Gun Trace Task Force, Justin Fenton, *The Baltimore Sun*, and Baynard Woods, *The Guardian* (page 246); coverage of Catherine Pugh's "Healthy Holly" scandal, *The Baltimore Sun* (page 247).

Acknowledgments

I T IS DIFFICULT TO LIMIT the number of people who deserve thanks, praise, and deepest appreciation for their support with the writing of this book and their support of me as I went through the process of telling these stories. The first people I have to thank are the eight people who shared their lives and their truths with me: Tawanda, John, Partee, Billy, Greg, Nick, John, and Jenny. Thank you, all of you, for letting your stories help the world understand those days—what led to them and what we learned from them. Your stories forced us to comprehend the stories of those we didn't profile individually in the book. The countless people who live in shadows or on society's fault lines. Those in poverty or near poverty. Those who fight and struggle every day under the weight of a system that is unfair. I thank you all because you have been not only a driving force behind this book, but inspirations in my life's work and purpose. You serve as an important reminder to push and not to be satisfied with, as Dr. King said, "the tranquilizing drug of gradualism."

To the mighty Chris Jackson and his entire One World

team, thank you for believing in this story from the very start. You continue to share your genius with the world and bring the ideas, thoughts, and opinions of your authors to a new level. I am honored to have you as my publishers, editors, marketing team, and allies in the work.

Linda Loewenthal, my agent extraordinaire, this book has been a process! But we walked together from start to finish and I am sincerely grateful. My family, my true alpha and omega, thank you. You gave me space not only to write but to reflect, and you served as a consistent motivation, making clear to me why getting this story done, and done right, mattered. Dawn, I have no greater fighter in my corner and my appreciation for you is boundless. Thank you, for life, for all you are. Mia and James, my prince and princess, everything I do, all day and every day, is to make you happy and proud. I hope this book, and the impact I pray it inspires, does that. To my mom, Joy Moore, and sisters, Shani and Nikki, you are my squad! Thank you for always believing and being there for me no matter what. I promise to always do the same for you. And to the rest of my family, you are with me no matter where you are. You love me no matter what, and that means more than you know.

This book could have not been completed without my Robin Hood team having my back and my flanks. You are some of the most committed group of poverty fighters I know, and your commitment to the work and to real results is inspiring. A particular shout-out to Sam Tweedy, Brian Jones, and Jason Cone, who reminded me every day that this was about much more than five days— it's about life's work, and it touches on the lives we fight to impact every day. In the words of the Joni Mitchell song "A Case of You," "I'm drawn to those ones that ain't afraid. I remember that time you told me, you said love is touching souls. Surely you touched mine. 'Cause part of you pours out of me in these lines from time to time." From the team to the board to the Leadership Council to our army of supporters, thank you, and hallelujah. To my friends Derek Kaufman and David Roberts: you viewed countless drafts and gave imperative feedback—your fingerprints are all over these pages. Thank you for pushing me to be bold in my words and recommendations. And Fagan Harris: your genius ran alongside me from day one. Thank you for taking this journey together with me. I could not have crossed the finish line without you.

My friends and anchors have consistently held me down, and I am deeply appreciative. My Baltimore family, who always made sure I remembered where I was from, but also made sure where I was from remembered me—we did this together, and all of you should be proud. My brothers Jeff Johnson, Zac McDaniels, Rev. Ron Owens, Rev. Jerome Stephens, Rev. Frank Reid, Rev. Donté Hickman, Rev. Todd Yeary, Rev. Harold Carter, John Willis, Luke Cooper, Lester Davis, D. Watkins, Matthew Jablow, Hassan Murphy, Chris Wilson, Ben Jealous, Guy Filippelli, Donald Davis, and Tom Geddes, and sisters Carla Hopkins, Tisha Edwards, Billie Malcolm, Ruth Ann Norton, Rachel Monroe, Sonja Santelises, Shanaysha Sauls, Catalina Byrd, and Dana DiCarlo—all of you at various times read drafts and provided insights, groundbreaking research, helpful criticism, and needed encouragement to go on and continue to tell this story. A special shout-out to my BridgeEdU team for enduring this even as we were building something to prevent tragedies like this from ever having to happen again, particularly to Kristen Mitsinikos for helping to put together the initial concept paper. And I would like to thank Baltimore organizations—like Baltimore

Corps, Leaders of a Beautiful Struggle, the Baltimore Algebra Project, Art with a Heart, Thread, and Writers in Baltimore Schools—whose support of the city's youth has made the city stronger and, importantly, let our youth lead.

My family extends far beyond Baltimore, and I can't forget those outside the city by the bay who were invaluable in helping this story get done: Phillip Banks, Ray McGuire, Robert Reffkin, Tony and Robyn Coles, Chuck Phillips and the entire Black Economic Alliance family, Tony and Bea Welters, Darrell Friedman, Dia Simms, Ericka Pittman, Tonya Carr, Toni Bias, Justin Brandon, Tommy Ransom, Lois Peters, Howard and Pam Thomas, Ralph and Donna Thomas, Pandora Flythe, Earl and Rita Flythe, Michelle Drayton, Valerie Drayton, Declan and Marissa Smalley, and Derek and Kendra Ausby.

To Erica L. Green, my friend and the person I believed could really bring this process to a proper and God-honoring close, I am thankful you said yes, and thankful for the final result, which you beautifully helped bring out. And Emily Krieger, whose fact checking made sure that the stories told reflected the truth of the moment and of these journeys.

Lastly but not at all least, to the family of Freddie Gray. One can only imagine the pain you all felt those days, and the pain you continue to feel. We honor you and your appreciation that your son, brother, cousin, et cetera, should change the world in death the way the world did not let him in life.

ERICA L. GREEN:

I would like to thank my family, the Burns, the Girardis, and the Simons, whose unconditional love, support, and patience sustain me in this life and my career. Thank you to Matt, Everly and Ezra, and Miriam for providing the foundation that makes all other things possible. To my vast network of friends, thank you for being the wind beneath my wings. Thank you to the educators, families, and students in the Baltimore City Public School System for making me a journalist.

This book would not be possible without my newspaper family at *The Baltimore Sun*, namely the Pulitzer-recognized team whose unparalleled coverage of Freddie Gray's death and its aftermath exemplified the bedrock principles of journalism and professionalism, and the commitment that newspapers have to their communities. Thank you to the *Sun*'s leaders and editors, Trif Alatzas, Sam Davis, Sean Welsh, Kalani Gordon, Laura Smitherman, Dave Rosenthal, Jen Badie, and Richard Martin, who steered the team through an extraordinary story with courage and grace. And thank you to Mary Corey for your legacy and guidance.

One of the true honors of my life was reporting on the front lines of Baltimore history alongside some of the most talented and tireless journalists in the business, many of whom I am also lucky to call friends. Among them: Liz Bowie, Yvonne Wenger, Luke Broadwater, Scott Dance, Justin Fenton, Justin George, Kevin Rector, Julie Scharper, Andy Green, Erin Cox, Colin Campbell, Ian Duncan, Doug Donovan, Jean Marbella, Dan Rodricks, and the entire photo staff, including Jeff Bill, Jerry Jackson, Lloyd Fox, Kim Hairston, Karl Ferron, Christopher Assaf, and Amy Davis.

To the reporters and editors who continue to make the *Sun* one of the most important papers in the country—Talia Richman, Tim Prudente, Diana Sugg, Tricia Bishop, Andrea McDaniels, Alison Knezevich, Jessica Anderson, David Zurawik, Peter Jensen—thank you for shining a "Light for All," especially in the city's darkest days.

To the wider Baltimore press corps who provided dogged

coverage of the uprising—not just the event itself but what preceded it and its aftermath—thank you for working alongside us not just as competitors, but as a team of rivals committed to telling one of the most important stories of our time. This includes the city's dedicated broadcast journalists; the writers and photographers formerly of *Baltimore City Paper*, including Baynard Woods, Lisa Snowden-McCray, J. M. Giordano, and Brandon Soderberg; and Jaisal Noor of the Real News Network. And thank you to the journalists who continue to cover the city with limited resources but limitless heart, like the writers at *Baltimore Beat* and *Baltimore Brew*.

Thank you to journalists at national outlets like Alec MacGillis for continuing to keep Baltimore in the national consciousness, as a city emblematic of intractable challenges but worth believing in.

The work of all of these journalists served as invaluable research and context for this project. They ran toward the fires, dodged bricks, marched with protesters, challenged authority and narratives, covered Freddie's family with compassion, elevated the voices of marginalized communities, chronicled critical turning points in the city's history, and exposed the systems and policies that provided the necessary context to understand why the city rose up.

I would also like to acknowledge a group of strong black women whose friendship, leadership, and/or mentorship at different points in my career helped me to find my own voice. Thank you, La Jerne Cornish, Alicia Wilson, Edie House Foster, Nikkia Rowe, Tammy Turner, Tahirah Burley, Cpl. Betty Covington, Tammatha Woodhouse, Lorna Hanley, Khalilah Harris, Tanika Davis, Kelly Brewington, Maryann James-Daley, Monique Jones, and Nikole Hannah-Jones for reminding me to never dim my light.

To my support system at *The New York Times*, namely Elisabeth Bumiller, Jonathan Weisman, Rebecca Corbett, Matt Purdy, Scott Shane, Katie Benner, Julie Davis, Mikayla Bouchard, Emily Cochrane, Lauretta Charlton, Jaime Swanson, Margaret Ho, Coral Davenport, Katie Rogers, and Eliza Shapiro, and the many, many others who have lent an ear, advice, and kind words: thank you for encouraging me to stay true to who I am, and for believing in me more than I believe in myself.

And finally, thank you to the children of Baltimore City for all that you are and will become.

Index

ABOUT THE AUTHORS

WES MOORE is the CEO of the Robin Hood Foundation, one of the largest anti-poverty organizations in the country. His first book, *The Other Wes Moore*, was a *New York Times* and *Wall Street Journal* bestseller; his second book, *The Work*, was also a bestseller and was featured on Oprah Winfrey's *SuperSoul Sunday*. Moore appears regularly as a commentator on NBC News. He lives in his hometown of Baltimore with his wife and two children.

robinhood.org/wes-moore/
Twitter: @iamwesmoore
Instagram: @iamwesmoore

ERICA L. GREEN is an award-winning journalist at *The New York Times*. She was previously a reporter at *The Baltimore Sun*, where she was part of the *Sun* team named a 2016 Pulitzer Prize finalist for breaking news coverage of the death of Freddie Gray.

Twitter: @EricaLG

ABOUT THE TYPE

This book was set in a Monotype face called Bell. John Bell (1745–1831) was responsible for the original cutting of this design. The vocations of Bell were many—bookseller, printer, publisher, typefounder, and journalist, among others. His types were considerably influenced by the delicacy and beauty of the French copperplate engravers. Monotype Bell might also be classified as a delicate and refined rendering of Scotch Roman.